STUDIES IN AFRICAN LITERATURE

Homecoming

STUDIES IN AFRICAN LITERATURE

A Reader's Guide to African Literature: HANS ZELL and HELENE SILVER
Homecoming: Essays: NGUGI WA THIONG'O
Writers in Politics: NGUGI WA THIONG'O
Morning Yet on Creation Day: CHINUA ACHEBE
African Literature in the Twentieth Century: O. R. DATHORNE
Protest and Conflict in African Literature
    Edited by COSMO PIETERSE and DONALD MUNRO
An Introduction to the African Novel: EUSTACE PALMER
The Growth of the African Novel: EUSTACE PALMER
The Novel and Contemporary Experience in Africa: ARTHUR SHATTO GAKWANDI
The Literature and Thought of Modern Africa: CLAUDE WAUTHIER
New West African Literature: KOLAWOLE OGUNGBESAN
The African Experience in Literature and Ideology: ABIOLA IRELE
Aspects of South African Literature
    Edited by CHRISTOPHER HEYWOOD
African Art and Literature: The Invisible Present: DENNIS DUERDEN
Four Centuries of Swahili Verse: JAN KNAPPERT
African Writers Talking
    Edited by DENNIS DUERDEN and COSMO PIETERSE
African Writers on African Writing
    Edited by G. D. KILLAM
Tendi: J. W. T. ALLEN
The Writings of Chinua Achebe: G. D. KILLAM
The Writing of Wole Soyinka: ELDRED JONES
The Poetry of L. S. Senghor: S. O. MEZU
The Poetry of Okot p'Bitek: G. A. HERON
An Introduction to the Writings of Ngugi: G. D. KILLAM
The Novels of Ayi Kwei Armah: ROBERT FRASER
The Writings of Camara Laye: ADELE KING

Critical Perspectives

Critical Perspectives on Chinua Achebe
    Edited by CATHERINE INNES and BERNTH LINDFORS
Critical Perspectives on Amos Tutuola
    Edited by BERNTH LINDFORS
Critical Perspectives on V. S. Naipaul
    Edited by ROBERT HAMNER
Critical Perspectives on Nigerian Literatures
    Edited by BERNTH LINDFORS
Critical Perspectives on Wole Soyinka
    Edited by JAMES GIBBS
Critical Perspectives on Ngugi
    Edited by G. D. KILLAM
Critical Perspectives on Christopher Okigbo
    Edited by D. NWOGA

African Literature Today

    Edited by ELDRED DUROSIMI JONES
1–4 Omnibus edition
  5 The Novel in Africa
  6 Poetry in Africa
  7 Focus on Criticism
  8 Drama in Africa
  9 Africa, America and the Caribbean
10 Retrospect and Prospect
11 Myth and History
12 New Writing, New Approaches

Homecoming

ESSAYS ON AFRICAN AND CARIBBEAN
LITERATURE, CULTURE AND POLITICS

NGUGI
WA THIONG'O

HEINEMANN
LONDON · IBADAN · NAIROBI

Heinemann Educational Books Ltd
22 Bedford Square, London WC1B 3HH
P.M.B. 5205 Ibadan · P.O.B. 45314 Nairobi
EDINBURGH MELBOURNE AUCKLAND
HONG KONG SINGAPORE KUALA LUMPUR
EXETER (NH) KINGSTON NEW DELHI
PORT OF SPAIN

ISBN 0 435 91750 1

Printed in Great Britain by
Biddles Ltd, Guildford, Surrey

Contents

I would like to thank:

REVEREND JOHN GATU
NGIGI NJONJO
MAINA WA KINYATTI
PIO ZIRIMU
NGATHO MUTHUMU
GRANT KAMENJU

and many friends whose provocative
discussions are always frank, free, and
fruitful.

Foreword

by IME IKIDDEH

▼▼▼▼▼▼▼▼▼▼▼▼▼▼▼▼▼▼▼▼▼▼▼▼▼▼▼▼▼▼▼▼▼

'I am not a man of the Church. I am not even a Christian.' Those were the stunning words with which James Ngugi opened his talk to the Fifth General Assembly of the Presbyterian Church of East Africa in Nairobi in March 1970, reproduced in this collection as *Church, Culture and Politics*. He had hardly ended his address when a wiry old man visibly choking with anger leapt to the floor, and, shaking his walking-stick menacingly towards the front, warned the speaker to seek immediate repentance in prayer. The old man did not forget to add as a reminder that in spite of his shameless denial and all his blasphemy, the speaker *was* a Christian, and the evidence was his first name. Ngugi had never given serious thought to this contradiction. Now it struck him that perhaps the old man had a point, and the name James, an unfortunate anomaly, had to go. This volume of essays is James Ngugi's first major publication under his new name. Those who might retort with 'What's in a name?' should ask themselves why several African countries have changed their names during the last fifteen years, and why in the Republic of Zaïre (itself a recent adoption) a name-changing revolution has swept through an entire Cabinet. The change in Ngugi's name is in itself perhaps of little consequence. What lends it some importance for our purpose is its significance in the wider context of the writer's beliefs, particularly as the heresy which shocked the Presbyterian congregation in Nairobi forms an essential part of those beliefs. This foreword cannot attempt a detailed evaluation of Ngugi's thought. What it seeks to do is merely to direct the reader's attention to some of its major features as revealed by these essays, and offer a few background comments in addition towards a richer appreciation not only of the essays themselves but also of the writer's creative work.

It will be seen that although the essays are grouped under three separate sections, they are vitally linked up by their dominant concerns, which are, put rather imperfectly and with particular reference to Africa: the confusion in values that has resulted from a drastic historical change in the political, economic and cultural ethos; the effect of such confusion on both society and the individual psyche; and the need to retain what is ours and recreate from it a new set of living values. The point of departure is the beginning of colonial rule and Christian missionary activity, with a reaching back to the slave trade seen as the earlier and more barbaric form of colonialism. In short, Ngugi is concerned here with the very subjects that have dominated African writing and the utterances of our more sensitive nationalist leaders for about half a century. Colonialism and capitalism are identified here as twin brothers whose mission is to exploit the material wealth of subject peoples, and who, in order to gain acceptability and perpetuation, enlist the services of their more sly but attractive first cousins, Christianity and Christian-oriented education, whose duty it is to capture the soul and the mind as well. Thus, history and values are distorted and reversed, and social order, disrupted beyond recognition, is replaced by another that is both foreign and unjust. With local variations, the African story is the same for Asia, the Caribbean and Latin America. It then becomes in these places a betrayal of trust by an indigenous élite, that has taken over power with the active support of the people, to continue the same inequitable system as the colonial oppressors. Two essays, 'Church, Culture and Politics' and 'The Novelist and his Past' carry the burden of this argument.

These essays are packed with an interest that goes beyond the writer's repetition of old themes. Here, freed from the limitations of fiction – for there are limits to what a writer can create and to what he can meaningfully communicate through fiction – Ngugi can make explicit statements informed and carried through by a passion and intellect which are only in circumscribed evidence in his best creative work. Most of the essays are dialectical in approach, and yet their messages remain at all times unambiguous and direct. They are often erudite without meaning to be so, and differ from the novels in dimension, in tone, and in the clarity of commitment. The fire that so often blazes within them is lit by indignation whose burning base is total conviction. Whatever critics might think of the preoccupations of these essays, it remains true that there can be no end to the discussion of the African encounter with Europe, because the wounds inflicted touched the very springs of life and have remained unhealed because they are constantly being gashed open again with more subtle, more lethal weapons. In any case, as an African who grew up in Kenya during the most turbulent days of that country's colonial history and who is now living through its aftermath, Ngugi's sentiments should surprise no one.

In order to clear up any doubts that may arise, two points of a background nature may be helpful here. The first has to do with Ngugi's Marxist thinking. One cannot go very far in these essays without being assailed by well-known phrases like 'the ruling classes' and 'the exploited peasant masses and urban workers', but if anyone regards these as empty traditional slogans then he cannot have known much of the history of Kenya. The irony is that it was the experience of social and economic relations in Britain, more than in Kenya, that actually settled Ngugi's socialist conviction. Starting from a commonsense appraisal of the situation in his country at independence, in particular, the need for a redistribution of land in the interests of a deprived peasantry. Ngugi arrived in England in 1964 and settled into the revolutionary atmosphere of Leeds University where he studied for the next few years. Extensive travels around Britain and Europe, acquaintance with some eminent British socialist scholars, including his supervisor, Dr Arnold Kettle, and discussions with the radical student group led by Alan Hunt – these revealed that the root cause of incessant industrial strife in Britain was no more than the old inter-class hostility inherent in the capitalist system. Thus Leeds provided an ideological framework for opinions that he already vaguely held. It was at this time too that we both read two books which became major influences: Frantz Fanon's *The Wretched of the Earth*, that classic analysis of the psychology of colonialism; and Robert Tressell's *The Ragged Trousered Philanthropists*, one of the most moving stories ever told of the plight of the working class in Britain. Echoes of Fanon are to be heard in some of these essays.

But although Ngugi sympathizes with the Marxist idea of the 'workers of the world', it is important to point out that he sees the experience of the black man as being unique in the world and as having a certain basic unity. He has re-emphasized this in a recent letter to me dated 4 September 1971 in which he writes:

> . . . for I believe that we as blacks have suffered doubly under colonialism and capitalism, first, as part of all the working masses, and then as blacks. By which I mean that a white worker by the very nature of his position was a beneficiary of the colonialist and racist exploitation of Africa and of black people everywhere.

This forms part of what he has described as the 'black dimension' to his beliefs, and a year's stay in the United States between 1970 and 1971 more than confirmed his views.

The origins of the 'black dimension' are to be seen in Ngugi's early interest in the Caribbean which he mentions in the essay 'A Kind of Homecoming'. That interest led him between 1965 and 1967 into an intensive research into the literature of the West Indies, an exercise which yielded the essays on the Caribbean in this volume. If the Caribbean essays exhibit a certain learned quality which many of the others do not, it is because they are the product of what was a scholarly research. The writer in fact would place little value on that quality. What was of greater importance to him was his discovery, through the novels he studied, of Africa's dominant presence in the West Indian consciousness, of the writers' agonizing sense of exile and persistent groping for some form of cultural identity. Ngugi's study does not stop with writers of African descent; it includes, for example, V. S. Naipaul whose attitude to the cultural problem in the Caribbean is cynical, often condescending and contemptuous. I think Ngugi interprets Naipaul with more seriousness than he deserves. But this by no means invalidates the kinship of the experience avowed by writers like Lamming, Braithwaite and Patterson.

It should be clear that Ngugi's conception of society is of a complex in which politics, economics and culture are inextricably tied up, and nowhere on that spectrum can he see capitalism offering any hope of progress and social justice that can be said to be accessible to all. In a post-colonial society and in a setting which in doctrine and practice runs counter to traditional communal values and works against the total involvement of the people in what is theirs, capitalism has nothing to recommend it. In that short talk to Makerere students, 'The Writer in a Changing Society', which incidentally brings together all the major themes of his novels, play and short stories, he is in fact recommending a socialist programme as the ideal means of harnessing all African aspirations when he says: 'For we must strive for a form of social organization which will free the manacled spirit and energy of our people so we can build a new country, and sing a new song.'

It is in this light, although he is not offering a new philosophy, that Ngugi must be seen as a writer who is also a thinker, and whose depth of thought and degree of commitment are yet to be attained by many African writers. These essays reveal a militancy not commonly associated with his creative work. It is of interest that his appreciation of other African writers in this volume is from the point of view of their apprehension of the African problem and what serious hope they can offer for the well-being of their society. Ngugi's great strength lies in his realization that in the search for social well-being, questions arising from the experience of yesterday must lead to a consideration of the here-and-now as a basis of hope for the yet-to-come. Not only 'where the rain began to beat us' and how severely, but also how to save ourselves from perpetual exposure, and our house from flood.

University of Ife
Nigeria

Author's Note

The present collection of essays is an integral part of the fictional world of *The River Between*, *Weep Not Child*, and *A Grain of Wheat*. Most of them were written at about the same time as the novels; they have been products of the same moods and touch on similar questions and problems. There are differences. In a novel the writer is totally immersed in a world of imagination which is other than his conscious self. At his most intense and creative the writer is transfigured, he is possessed, he becomes a medium. In the essay the writer can be more direct, didactic, polemical, or he can merely state his beliefs and faith: his conscious self is here more at work. Nevertheless the boundaries of his imagination are limited by the writer's beliefs, interests, and experiences in life, by where in fact he stands in the world of social relations. This must be part of the reason that readers are curious about a writer's opinion on almost everything under the sun – from politics and religion to conservation of wild life! The writer is thus forced either by the public or by the needs of his craft to define his beliefs, attitudes and outlook in the more argumentative form of the essay.

Two things I might here explain: the emphasis, in this collection, is on politics and on West Indian fiction. Literature does not grow or develop in a vacuum; it is given impetus, shape, direction and even area of concern by social, political and economic forces in a particular society. The relationship between creative literature and these other forces cannot be ignored, especially in Africa, where modern literature has grown against the gory background of European imperialism and its changing manifestations: slavery, colonialism and neo-colonialism. Our culture over the last hundred years has developed against the same stunting, dwarfing background.

There is no area of our lives which has not been affected by the social, political and expansionist needs of European capitalism: from that of the reluctant African, driven by whips and gunpowder to work on the cotton plantations of America, the rubber plantations in the Congo, the gold and diamond mines in southern Africa, to that of the modern African worker spending his meagre hard-earned income on imported cars and other goods (razor blades and Coca Cola even), to bolster the same

Western industries that got off the ground on the backs of his peasant ancestors and on the plunder of a continent. Yet the sad truth is that instead of breaking from an economic system whose life-blood is the wholesale exploitation of our continent and the murder of our people, most of our countries have adopted the same system. There has been little attempt at breaking with our inherited colonial past – our inherited economic and other institutions, apart from blackanizing the personnel running them. There has been no basic land reform; the settler owning 600 acres of land is replaced by a single African owning the same 600 acres. There has been no change in the structure and nature of ownership of various companies, banks and industries; the two or three European directors go away to be replaced by two or three indigenous directors – the companies remain foreign-owned. There has been no socialization of the middle commercial sector; the Asian dukawallah goes away, to be replaced by a single African dukawallah. There has not been much structural reform of the educational system; the former white schools remain as special high standard schools, attended only by those who can afford the exorbitant fees. Of course there have been advances: our destiny is now in our own hands. And much has been done – much is still being done – even within stifling, inherited systems. But the lack of structural transformation of our societies means that our economies and other institutions will continue, as in the past, to be tied to the West. We shall then end up being just mediators between Western cities and African villages. Do we think that Western capitalism and the classes that run it have suddenly changed their motives and interests in Africa? Aid, loans, Oxfam and other freedom from hunger campaigns – where has this disinterested philanthropy, not manifest when Europe was in actual political control of Africa, suddenly emerged from? What Norman Leys in his book *Kenya* said of the supposed change of the Kenya settlers' attitude to Africans (under the pressure of the Indian challenge for equality, the white settlers suddenly discovered they and they alone could protect the African from the Indian menace) can be said of the Western interests and motives behind their desire to protect Africa from socialism!

> I, on the contrary, cannot forget what these same men did and permitted to be done when they had things all their own way, and I mistrust a change of heart that conflicts with people's strongest interests and long cherished and dearest ambitions.

Literature is of course primarily concerned with what any political and economic arrangement does to the spirit and the values governing human relationships. Nobody who has passed through the major cities of Europe and America, where capitalism is in full bloom, can ever wish the same fate on Africa – as far as human relationships are concerned. He cannot have failed to see the abject poverty, the moral and physical degradation, and the cultural impoverishment of large masses of the population – amidst plenty and luxury enjoyed by so few. We would be deceiving ourselves if we thought that indigenous capitalism – even if it could develop outside the orbit of international monopoly capitalism and former colonial masters to a competitive level – would produce a society where a few, even if they are black, do not live on the blood of others. For it is not simply a question of some people, be they black, yellow or red, being more wicked or less moral than others. The system we have chosen has its own inexorable logic. While riding roughshod on a people's most cherished institutions and culture, capitalism and the competitive accumulation of private property and profit encourages the most reactionary, clannish, and regional feelings which keep the exploited disunited. Every hunter must dread the thought of what would happen if the hunted were ever to unite.

Today, in Africa, we are harvesting the bitter fruits of capitalist and colonialist policy of divide and rule, and those of the colonial legacy of an uneven development, i.e. the current murderous suspicion and hatred between the various national groups and regions. It is easy to see how these élitist-created feuds come about. There has been no radical change in the inherited structures and in our priorities, too few openings in business, civil service and professional hierarchies, and the competition for these few openings becomes very fierce. An alliance of business, civil service, professional and political élites of each linguistic group feel their positions threatened and jeopardized by their counterparts in other national groups. The top few quickly identify their interests with the interests of the whole cultural linguistic group and cry wolf! The wolf here is another tribe or a supposed combination of other tribes. Yet a cursory glance around would show there are no tribes in Africa – the economic and social forces that gave rise to various nations in pre-colonial Africa have collapsed. What is left is only a linguistic cultural superstructure into which Western education aided by the colonial spiritual police (i.e. the missionaries) have made many inroads.

'Tribe' is a special creation of the colonial regimes. Now there are only two tribes left in Africa: the 'haves' and the 'have nots'. What goes for tribalism in Africa is really a form of civil war among the 'haves', struggling for crumbs from the masters' tables. The masters sit in New York, London, Brussels, Paris, Bonn and Copenhagen; they are the owners of the oil companies, the mines, the banks, the breweries, the insurance institutions – all the moving levers of the economy. It is this situation that has given us

A Man of the People, Song of Lawino, Voices in the Dark. It is this that is behind the critical self-appraisal and the despair in much of the current African literature. Few contemporary novels can match the bitterness in Armah's *The Beautyful Ones Are Not Yet Born*:

> So this was the real gain. The only real gain. This was the thing for which poor men had fought and shouted. This is what it had come to: not that the whole thing might be overturned and ended, but that a few blackmen might be pushed closer to their masters, to eat some of the fat into their bellies too. That had been the entire end of it all.

It is the height of irony that we, who have suffered most from exploitation, are now supporting a system that not only continues that basic exploitation, but exacerbates destructive rivalries between brothers and sisters, a system that thrives on the survival instincts of dwellers in a Darwinian jungle. The writer cannot be exempted from the task of exposing the distorted values governing such a jungle precisely because this distorts healthy human relationships.

To turn briefly to the other main topic in this book, my interest in West Indian literature started as a personal passion; but this has now been buttressed by my belief in the basic unity of the black experience and the necessity of unity in the black world. We have the same biological and geographic origins; we have suffered the same colonial fate (slavery, colonialism, neo-colonialism). We have similar objective aspirations: to be culturally and economically free so that we can restore the creative glory of Africa and of all Africans. For this we need a system that calls out the best and the most creative in us. Yet it is another sad truth that the forces which have militated against continental and even national unity are the same ones that have kept black peoples disunited, for they want to remain arbiters between African peoples. Africans abroad have been fed on the myth of Tarzan's Africa, and we too have been fed on the myth of 'negroes', who have lost all links and interest in Africa. Some of these people, once described by Jomo Kenyatta as professional friends and interpreters of the African, have the arrogance of assuming that they have more and closer natural ties to Africa than have Africans in the West Indies and in America. It is such people who acquire a most proprietorial air when talking of the part of Africa they have happened to visit; they carve a personal sphere of influence and champion the most reactionary and the most separatist cause of whichever group among whom they happen to live. They are again the most vehement in pointing out the unique intelligence, amiability and quick wit of their adopted areas and groups. We must never succumb to the poisonous and divisive flattery of our enemies. We must find for ourselves what are the most enduring links between us and all our brothers scattered over the world. We can then build on these links, build a socialist black power.

I hope the running themes in the present collection will raise questions and promote debate about our present predicament. For we are all involved in a common problem: how best to build a true communal home for all Africans. Then all the black people, all the African masses can truthfully say: we have come home.

NGUGI WA THIONG'O
University of Nairobi

Part One: On Culture

Towards a National Culture[1]

'The claim to a national culture in the past does not only rehabilitate that nation and serve as a justification for the hope of a future national culture. In the sphere of psycho-affective equilibrium it is responsible for an important change in the native.'

Frantz Fanon

I was asked some time ago to make a small study of 'the ways in which African countries can open up their traditional structures to the modern world while preserving and developing their original cultures'. This statement contains questionable assumptions. It implies, first, that African traditional structures and cultures have been unaffected by the march of history and have remained closed to the rest of the world. Yet it is self-evident that Africa's political and economic structures were seriously disrupted by colonialism, which brought in its wake innovations in education, religion and medicine. Moreover, Africa has contributed much to the development of the rest of the world through centuries of trade and conquest. It also should not be forgotten that it was African labour and Africa's material wealth that built America and the major cities of Europe. African sculpture has decisively influenced that of Europe: a collection of African art will be found in the major museums of the world. We know also that jazz, with its now wide influence on modern music, is derived from African rhythms and musical art-forms. Even Western scholars are beginning to reject Hegel's heresy – that Africa proper, for all purposes of connection with the rest of the world, had remained shut up. Herskovits has been one of those at the forefront of this new approach:

Africa, when seen in perspective, was a full partner in the development of the Old World, participating in a continual process of cultural give-and-take that began long before European occupation. Neither isolation nor stagnation tell the tale. It is as incorrect to think of Africa as having been for centuries isolated from the rest of the world as it is to regard the vast area south of the Sahara as 'Darkest Africa', whose peoples slumbered on until awakened by the coming of the dynamic civilization of Europe . . . In [the] spread of culture, Africa was a donor as well as a recipient.[2]

Also questionable is the attitude towards culture that emerges from the statement. Is culture something which can be preserved, even if this were desirable? Is there such a thing as an original culture?

Culture, in its broadest sense, is a way of life fashioned by a people in their collective endeavour to live and come to terms with their total environment. It is the sum of their art, their science and all their social institutions, including their system of beliefs and rituals. In the course of this creative struggle and progress through history, there evolves a body of material and spiritual values which endow that society with a unique ethos. Such values are often expressed through the people's songs, dances, folk-lore, drawing, sculpture, rites and ceremonies. Over the years these varieties of artistic activity have come to symbolize the meaning of the word culture. Any discussion of culture inevitably centres around these activities, but we must bear in mind that *they* are derived from a people's way of life and will change as that way of life is altered, modified, or developed through the ages. In our present situation we must in fact try to see how new aspects of life can be clarified or given expression through new art-forms or a renewal of the old.

We need to see Africa's cultural history in three broad phases: Africa before white conquest, Africa under colonial domination, and today's Africa striving to find its true self-image. To do this is to indicate the obvious: that the pressures, inside and outside, at the different stages of her growing up have changed Africa's cultural needs and outlook. Yesterday, for instance, there were many ethnic groups, each with a distinct, cohesive culture: today, these groups are trying to form nations within wider, more inclusive boundaries of geography and politics. Hence we should examine the role of culture in our time within the new horizons, themselves made hazy by the often conflicting calls of the tribe, the nation, pan-Africa, and even the Third World.

Yet too often, as in the statement under discussion, we talk of African culture as if it were a static commodity which can and should be rescued from the ruins and shrines of yesterday, and projected on to a modern stage to be viewed by Africa's children, who, long lost in the labyrinth of foreign paths in an unknown forest, are now thirsty and hungry for the wholesome food of their forefathers. No living culture is ever static. Collectively, human beings struggle to master their physical environment and in the process create a social one. A change in the physical environment, or, more accurately, a change in the nature of their struggle, will alter their institutions and hence their mode of life and thought. Their new mode of life and thought may in turn affect their institutions and general environment. It is a dialectical process. A profound change in a people's economy, or in their dwelling-place, through trade and migration, will make people organize themselves differently to meet the new set of circumstances. Their ideals and values, over a period, are also likely to alter. We know that trade across the Sahara brought new ideas and technological innovations, with marked effects on some West African societies. The southward movement of people along the Nile turned some hitherto pastoral groups into tillers of the soil, demanding a new mode of life and system of values. Professor Ogot pinpoints one of these changes, that of the Luo attitude to land:

> The [Luo] people had . . . no great love for the land on which they lived, as long as there was enough of it for their cattle, and their crops . . . This traditional attitude to land has, however, changed – for two reasons. The southern migration of the Nilotes took some of the groups into forested or formerly forested areas where an agricultural economy was more suitable. The result is that the degree of the cattle complex in the Nilotic world decreases as one moves southwards from the Sudan . . . Most of the Kenya Luo, for example, who traditionally were much more attached to their flocks than to their fields are now much more attached to their fields and some are even prepared to do without their flocks . . . There was a growing sense of the value of land, and the result is that each family today is closely tied religiously and spiritually to the land of its ancestors.[3]

Contrary to the myth and fiction of our conquerors, Africa was always in a turmoil of change, with empires rising and falling. African traditional structures and cultures then were neither static nor uniform. There were as many cultures as there were peoples, although we can recognize broad affinities which would make us talk meaningfully of African values or civilizations.

Bearing this in mind, we can rightly ask ourselves about the attitude to artistic activities in traditional Africa. For convenience we should distinguish between the two categories of societies identified by M. Fortes and E. E. Evans-Pritchard:

> One group consists of those societies which have centralized authority, administrative machinery, and judicial institutions – and in which cleavages of wealth, privilege, and status correspond to the distribution

of power and authority . . . The other group consists of those societies which lack centralized authority, administrative machinery, and constituted judicial institutions – and in which there are no sharp divisions of rank, status or wealth.[4]

In the first group, for instance the Yorubas of Nigeria and the Baganda of Uganda, there was a more sharply defined social hierarchy, with a high degree of specialization of functions. The surplus from the farmers fed professional priests and priestesses (or political office-holders) tending the shrines of the people's gods, and professional sculptors and artisans in the courts of the great. In the other group, for instance the Ibo of Nigeria and the Agikuyu of Kenya, the rather loose, more egalitarian political set-up – though 'beneath the apparent fragmentation of authority lay deep fundamental unities'[5] in religious and cultural spheres – did not allow the same degree of specialization of functions. Political office did not carry economic privileges; it certainly did not confer on the holder power over the community's surplus or over the loot from war, to give him the ability to hire special followers and specialized skills to entertain him during his leisure and to further enhance his status. Among the Agikuyu, for instance, only a very tiny group of workers in metal lived wholly by their skill, exchanging their wares for food and clothes. Apart from these, the people tended their farms, and also played music, officiated in ceremonial dances, recited poetry and stories around the fireside, and became warriors in time of war.

However, in both types of societies art was functional; it was not, as it is in modern Europe, severed from the physical, social and religious needs of the community. Song, dance and music were an integral part of a community's wrestling with its environment, part and parcel of the needs and aspirations of the ordinary man. There was never, in any African society, the cult of the artist with its bohemian priests along the banks of Seine or Thames. Today the artist in Europe sees himself as an outsider, living in a kind of individual culture, and obeying only the laws of his imagination. This is the position of James Joyce's hero in *A Portrait of the Artist as a Young Man*:

> I will tell you what I will do and what I will not do. I will not serve that in which I no longer believe, whether it call itself my home, my fatherland or my church; and I will try to express myself in some mode of life or art as freely as I can and as wholly as I can, using for my defence the only arms I allow myself to use – silence, exile and cunning.[6]

Such an art ministers to a culture of the mind. It is the culture of Matthew

Arnold, who urged the English middle classes to strive for sweetness and light by knowing the best that had been thought and written in the world. Thereafter this individual man of culture could carry 'others along with him in his march towards perfection, to be continually doing all he can to enlarge and increase the volume of the human stream sweeping thitherward'.[7] Arnold's culture was an intellectual activity of the individual.

African Art, we can generally say, used to be oriented to the community. And because of its public nature, culture, in its broad as well as in the narrow sense, helped to weld society together. The integrative function of culture as described by W. E. Abrahams holds particularly true of traditional societies:

> Culture is an instrument for making (mutual) sufferance and co-operation natural. Its success depends on the extent to which it is allowed to be self-authenticating. Though it allows for internal discussion, and is indeed nourished thereby, the principles of decision in such discussions are themselves provided by culture. By uniting the people in common beliefs, actions and values, culture fills with order that portion of life which lies beyond the pale of state intervention . . . It fills it in such a way as at the same time to integrate its society, on the basis of common attitudes, common values. It creates the basis of the formulation of a common destiny and co-operation in pursuing it.[8]

Jomo Kenyatta's powerful book *Facing Mount Kenya* is a living example of this integrative function of culture. To read it is to witness a world with an inner, dynamic spirit; it is also an authentic refutation of the missionary condemnation of what they, the semi-gods, thought was savage and dark. After discussing all the aspects of Agikuyu life, Kenyatta concludes with an aggressive assertion of the primary role of culture in a people's discovery of their identity:

> It is all these aspects of life that make up a social culture. And it is the culture which he inherits that gives a man his human dignity as well as his material prosperity. It teaches him his mental and moral values and makes him feel it worthwhile to work and fight for liberty.[9]

It was these 'mental and moral' values that the European colonizer was bent on destroying in the classical tradition of Prospero. In the story of Prospero and Caliban, Shakespeare had dramatized the practice and psychology of colonization years before it became a global phenomenon. It is worth quoting the well-known scene between Prospero and Caliban:

CALIBAN: . . . When thou cam'st first,
    Thou strok'st me, and made much of me; wouldst give me
    Water with berries in't; and teach me how
    To name the bigger light, and how the less,
    That burn by day and night; and then I loved thee
    And shew'd thee all the qualities o' th' isle,
    And fresh springs, brine-pits, barren place and fertile.
    Cursed be I that did so! – All the charms
    Of Sycorax – toads, beetles, bats, light on you!
    For I am all the subjects that you have,
    Which first was mine own king; and here you sty me
    In this hard rock, whiles you do keep from me
    The rest o' th' island.

PROSPERO: Thou most lying slave,
    Whom stripes may move, not kindness! I have used thee
    (Filth as thou art) with humane care; and lodged thee
    In mine own cell till thou didst seek to violate
    The honour of my child . . .
    I pitied thee,
    Took pains to make thee speak, taught thee each hour
    One thing or other: when thou didst not, savage,
    Know thine own meaning, but wouldst gabble like
    A thing most brutish, I endow'd thy purposes
    With words that made them known: but thy vile race,
    Though thou didst learn, had that in't which good natures
    Could not abide to be with; therefore wast thou
    Deservedly confined into this rock, who hadst
    Deserved more than prison.[10]

Note that Propero had already admitted to his daughter that they cannot
do without Caliban, for:

    . . . he does make our fire,
    Fetch in our wood; and serves in offices
    That profit us.[11]

A number of things and attitudes emerge from the play. Prospero, the
stranger on the island, comes with the soft voice of the serpent. He is at
first friendly to Caliban, and flatters him, but all the time he is learning
the secrets of the island. To him Caliban has no culture or meaningful past.

He has even given *his* language to Caliban. And before Caliban knows it, Prospero has taken his land, has set up a one-man government, and turns Caliban into a slave-labourer. Ariel, formerly Caliban's subject, is released from bondage into a new servitude: he will only be finally freed if he remains Prospero's faithful servant and spy.

Like Prospero, the European colonizer instinctively knew and feared the threat posed by men with confidence in their own past and heritage. Why else should he devote his military might, his religious fervour, and his intellectual energy to denying that the African had true gods, had a culture, had a significant past? The missionary attacked the primitive rites, the dances, the graven images, recoiling from their suggestion of satanic sensuality. Some of the best minds of Europe abetted this grand deception.

Take Karen Blixen, for instance, who came from an aristocratic house in Denmark. She settled in Kenya and for thirteen years used her creative genius in farming and observing the natives and animals. She was once a possible candidate for a Nobel Prize for Literature, I suppose because of her truly astonishing conclusions:

> The natives of the land, the Kikuyu, Wakamba, Kavirondo and Masai, have got their old mysterious and simple cultural traditions, which seem to lose themselves in the darkness of very ancient days. We ourselves have carried European light to the country quite lately, but we have had the means to spread and establish it quickly.[12]

Of the intellectual capacity of the African she was even more original:

> The dark nations of Africa, strikingly precocious as young children, seemed to come to a standstill in their mental growth at different ages. The Kikuyu, Kavirondo and Wakamba, the people who worked for me on the farm, in early childhood were far ahead of white children of the same age, but they stopped quite suddenly at a stage corresponding to that of a European child of nine. The Somali had got further and had all the mentality of boys of our race at the age of 13 to 17.[13]

These kinds of attitudes had rich intellectual ancestry in Hegel, with his Africa, a land of childhood, lying beyond the days of self-conscious history and enveloped in the dark mantle of the night.

But what was of far-reaching effect was the fact that, again like Prospero, the European took away the material base, and systematically dismantled the political and economic institutions on which the African had built his way of life. In the 'egalitarian' societies, for instance, he imposed a chief, a central visible focus of authority, where none existed before. In the other category, he removed the base on which the central authority had rested: the source of political authority of the King was no longer the people from whom he demanded allegiance and to whom he also owed duties. But in both cases, the traditional institutions were allowed to remain only where they further facilitated the thorough exploitation of land in the settler colonies of the East and Central Africa, or the exploitation of raw materials and markets in the more commercial colonies of West Africa. By introducing an aggressive money-economy, and new educational and religious systems, while denying the African the economic and political power by which he could control them, the European colonialist 'put a knife on the things that held us together and we have fallen apart'.[14]

The effect of the colonial presence was to create an élite who took on the tongue and adopted the style of the conquerors. They hearkened to the voice of the missionary's God, cried Hallelujah, and raised their eyes to Heaven. They derided the old gods and they too recoiled with a studied (or genuine) horror from the primitive rites of their people. The rest, for the colonial system by its very nature has room only for a few, were often deprived of their land and then herded into the settlers' farms, or to urban centres to become hewers of wood and drawers of water. The first group lost contact with their roots. They despised anything that smelt of the primitive past. It is this group mostly whom Achebe must have had in mind when he cried: 'If I were god, I would regard as the very worst our acceptance – for whatever reason – of racial inferiority.'[15] The other group remained close to the soil and never completely lost contact with their traditions. The resilience of African culture was somehow able to withstand a certain amount of battering and propaganda. It is difficult, as Prospero found out, for colonial domination to completely crush the human spirit. In the struggle for independence the peasants and often the urban workers invoked their ancestral gods for strength to fight the foe. They adapted traditional rhythms, songs and dances to the new needs of the struggle. The intellectuals, the élite, the middle classes also found themselves not quite accepted in the world of the conquerors. Rejected by their counter-parts in the white structure, their humanity sometimes denied in the name of race, they were as it were thrown back on to the masses. They started to reclaim their past, often with bitter nostalgia. Alioune Diop declared at the first World Conference of Negro Writers and Artists in Paris:

There is this scandalous allegation of peoples without culture. While it is true that those who were really responsible for colonization knowingly fabricated this myth, it is none the less surprising that generations of cultural and spiritual authorities have conceded that men could live in a community without culture.[16]

Because he knew that this 'scandalous allegation' was also embodied in European books, especially fiction, on Africa, the African writer tried to answer by asserting in the books he wrote that Africa had a culture as good as any. The Negritude movement was a cultural phenomenon with a political facet. It was generally realized that a community deprived of its political liberty would find it difficult to recreate an image of its past and confidently look towards the future.

The realization was general, at times vague. The belief has persisted, among most African intellectuals, artists and politicians, that 'cultural liberation is an essential condition for political liberation'.[17] And since they think of culture only in terms of dances, jungle drums and folk-lore, they think it enough if they assert the need for the revival of these things. But it is wrong to think of culture as prior to politics. Political and economic liberation are the essential condition for cultural liberation, for the true release of a people's creative spirit and imagination. It is when people are involved in the active work of destroying an inhibitive social structure and building a new one that they begin to see themselves. They are born again. In traditional Africa we have seen how culture, as a mode of life, was intimately bound up with the social fabric, which was based on man's relationship to the land. The colonialist knew this. We have pointed out that his pooh-poohing of the African way of life went hand in hand with a deliberate destruction of the material base on which it was built:

> A culture has no meaning apart from the social organisation of life on which it is built. When the European comes to Gikuyu country and robs the people of their land, he is taking away not only their livelihood, but the material symbol that holds family and tribe together. In doing this he gives one blow which cuts away the foundations from the whole Gikuyu life, social moral and economic.[18]

The Kenya colonial struggle centred round the demand for the lost lands. Suddenly, in the course of demanding this, while some died and others refused to give up, the Kenyan peasantry seemed to find a new power. They rejected the missionary colonial institutions. They started building their own schools, and their own churches. They rediscovered the old songs – they had never completely lost touch with them – and reshaped them to meet the new needs of their struggle. They also created new songs and dances with new rhythms where the old ones were found inadequate.

Through Mau Mau, they organized themselves, in the villages, and in the towns, their vision going beyond the narrow confines of the tribe.

Today, after regaining their independence, most African countries are committed to developing a distinctive national culture. In some cases, they have even set up agencies to promote it. Yet little has been done to translate this commitment into action. This, in part, is due to wrong attitudes towards culture. There are people, honest people, who confuse culture with irrelevant traditionalism; it is surely not possible to lift traditional structures and cultures intact into modern Africa. A meaningful culture is the one born out of the present hopes and especially the hopes of an impoverished peasantry, and that of the growing body of urban workers. There are still other people who believe that you can somehow maintain colonial, economic, and other social institutions and graft on them an African culture. We have seen that colonial institutions can only produce a colonial mentality. The trouble, of course, is that many African middle classes helped to smother the revolutionary demands of the majority of peasants and workers and negotiated a treaty of mutual trust with the white colonial power structure. In fighting for independence, some of the African intelligentsia only wanted that which was forbidden to them, or rather they saw the struggle in terms of their immediate needs, nurtured by the social position they had attained under the colonial system, whose fulfilment was however frustrated by the racism inherent in the system. They wanted to wear the same clothes and shoes, get the same salary, live in the same kind of mansions as their white counterparts of similar qualifications. After independence, the racial barrier to their needs was broken. The gold-rush for the style of living of their former conquerors had started. Skin-lighteners, straightened hair, irrelevant drawing-room parties, conspicuous consumption in the form of country villas, Mercedes-Benzes and Bentleys, were the order of the day. Clutching their glasses of whisky and soda, patting their wigs delicately lest they fall, some of these people will, in the course of cocktail parties, sing a few traditional songs: hymns of praise to a mythical past: we must preserve our culture, don't you think?

If we are to achieve true national cultures we must recognize our situation. That means we must thoroughly examine our social and economic structures and see if they are truly geared to meeting the needs and releasing the energy of the masses. We must in fact wholly Africanize and socialize our political and economic life. We must break with capitalism, whose imperialistic stage – that of colonialism and neo-colonialism – has done so much harm to Africa and dwarfed our total creative spirit. Capitalism can only produce anti-human culture, or a culture that is only an expression of sectional, warring interests. African culture used to be most communal

when and where economic life and the means of production were commmu-
nally organized and controlled. Any ideal, any vision, is nothing unless it
is given institutional forms and solid economic bases. This recognition is
at the heart of the now famous Arusha declaration in Tanzania. The
declaration shows that Tanzanians are aware that most African countries,
though independent in name, are still in a semi-colonial state:

> We have been oppressed a great deal, we have been exploited a great
> deal and we have been degraded a great deal. It is our weakness that
> has led to our being oppressed, exploited, disregarded. Now we want a
> revolution – a revolution which brings to an end our weakness so that
> we are never again exploited, oppressed and humiliated.[19]

And they know that no revolution has ever been brought about by pious
hopes and dreams. People evolve culture through practical labour, through
production of their means of living. The kind of culture that emerges will
depend on how people collectively organize their resources:

> Tanzania is a nation of peasants and workers, but it is not yet a socialist
> society. It still contains elements of feudalism and capitalism – with
> their temptations. These feudalistic and capitalistic features of our
> society could spread and entrench themselves . . . To build and maintain
> socialism it is essential that all the major means of production and
> exchange in the nation are controlled and owned by the peasants through
> the machinery of their government and their cooperatives. Further, it
> is essential that the ruling Party should be a Party of peasants and
> workers.[20]

In other words, Tanzania is giving back to the peasants and workers the
material basis in which they can build a new and modern national culture.

My thesis, when we come to today's Africa, is then very simple: a
completely socialized economy, collectively owned and controlled by the
people, is necessary for a national culture: a complete and total liberation
of the people, through the elimination of all exploitative forces, is necessary for a national culture. A stratified society, even in pre-colonial Africa,
produces a stratified culture or a sub-cultures, sometimes to the total
exclusion from the central hub of national life of the *ahois*, the *ndungatas*,
the *osus*, the *mbaras*, the slaves and serfs in such pre-colonial societies, and
of the peasantry and working people in modern neo-colonial states. An
oppressive racist society, like that of South Africa, can only produce an
oppressive racist culture that cannot nourish and edify man.

While ultimately the development of a meaningful self-image is dependent on the complete re-structuring of our societies, we must also create practical, specific policies to facilitate the emergence of new attitudes and art-forms. One example will do: the educational policy (as it relates to literature and art).

The colonial system produced the kind of education which nurtured subservience, self-hatred, and mutual suspicion. It produced a people uprooted from the masses. Often there was racial discrimination in the allocation of schools, of teachers, of teaching facilities. In the whole of East, Central and South Africa, for instance, there were schools for Europeans, for Asians and for Africans. There were even toilets for Europeans, for Asians, and then for Africans. Society was a racial pyramid: the European minority at the top, the Asian in the middle, and the African forming the base. The educational system reflected this inequality. It encouraged a slave mentality, with a reverent awe for the achievements of Europe. Europe was the centre of the universe. Africa was discovered by Europe: it was an extension of Europe. So in history people learnt about the rise of the Anglo-Saxons as if they were the true ancestors of the human race. Even in geography, the rocks of Europe had to be studied first before coming to Africa.

The destructive effect of colonial education, which sees Europe as the centre of the universe and man's history, is well illustrated in Sembène Ousmane's novel, *God's Bits of Wood*.[21] Education, for N'Deye, sets her apart from the struggle of her people for liberation and a betterment of living conditions. She dreams of love and she is utterly ashamed of her people and of herself:

The people among whom she lived were polygamous, and it had not taken her long to realize that this kind of union had nothing to do with love – at least not with love as she imagined it. And this, in turn, had made her recognize what she now called the 'lack of civilization' of her own people. In the books she had read, love was something that went with parties and costume balls, weekends in the country and trips in automobiles, yachting trips and vacations abroad, elegant anniversary presents and the fall showings at the great couturiers. Real life was there; not here, in this wretched corner, where she was confronted with beggars and cripples at every turning. When N'Deye came out of a theatre where she had seen visions of mountain chalets deep in snow, of beaches where the great of the world lay in the sun, of cities where the nights flashed with many-colored lights, and walked from this world back into her own, she would be seized with a kind of nausea, a mixture of rage and shame.

One day she had made a mistake on the date of a film she wanted to see and gone into a theatre where a documentary film on a tribe of Pygmies was being shown. She had felt as if she were being hurled backward, and down to the level of these dwarfs, and had an insane desire to run out of the theatre, crying aloud, 'No, no! These are not the real Africans!' And on another day, when a film of the ruins of the Parthenon appeared on the screen, two men seated behind her had begun talking loudly. N'Deye had turned on them like an avenging fury and cried in French, 'Be quiet, you ignorant fools! If you don't understand, get out!' N'Deye herself knew far more about Europe than she did about Africa; she had won the prize in geography several times in the years when she was going to school. But she had never read a book by an African author – she was quite sure that they could teach her nothing.

Today, the more blatant racial aspects of our education have been re-moved. But the actual educational system which aimed at producing subservient minds which at the same time looked down upon the rural peasantry and the urban workers has not been radically altered. In our schools, in our universities, Europe tends to be at the centre. And the emphasis has been on producing men born to rule!

Only the other day a very important controversy arose at the University of Nairobi, when a group of lecturers questioned the validity of an English Department, the only department concerned with literary studies, which continued teaching only British literature in the heart of independent Africa. This chauvinistic, basically colonial approach to the study of human-ities was justified on the grounds that people needed to study the historic continuity of a single culture! British of course! Underlying this was an assumption that the British traditions and the emergence of the modern West were the root of our consciousness and cultural heritage. The lecturers retorted:

Here is our main question: if there is need for a study of the historic continuity of a single culture, why can't this be African? Why can't African Literature be at the centre so that we can view other cultures in relationship to it? The aim in short should be to orientate ourselves towards placing Kenya, East Africa, then Africa in the centre. All other things are to be seen and considered in their relevance to our situation.[22]

Towards this end, they demanded the abolition of the English Department and the setting up, in its place, of a Department devoted mainly to African Literature and Languages. The Department of Literature would teach modern African writing in English and French, Afro-American and Caribbean Literature and a selected course in European literary tradition. But at the core of such a Department would be the study of oral tradition in African literature.

> The study of the Oral Tradition would . . . supplement (not replace) courses in Modern African Literature. By discovering and proclaiming loyalty to indigenous values, the new literature would on the one hand be set in the stream of history to which it belongs and so be better appreciated; and on the other be better able to embrace and assimilate other thoughts without losing its roots.[23]

Such a study would be important both in rehabilitating our minds, but also in helping African writers to innovate and break away from the European literary mainstream.

> [Already] one may note that African literature in the European languages lays claim to being differentiated from the metropolitan literatures not only in its content but also to some extent in its form. Its originality comes from the recourse made by our writers not only to African themes and subjects, and to elements of folklore, but also to stylistic innovations derived from the formal features of traditional African Literature.[24]

Equally important for our cultural renaissance is the teaching and study of African languages. We have already seen what any colonial system does: impose its tongue on the subject races, and then down-grade the vernacular tongues of the people. By so doing they make the acquisition of their tongue a status symbol; anyone who learns it begins to despise the peasant majority and their barbaric tongues. By acquiring the thought-processes and values of his adopted tongue, he becomes alienated from the values of his mother tongue, or from the language of the masses. Language after all is a carrier of values fashioned by a people over a period of time. It seems to me that in a country where ninety per cent speak African languages, it is very unwise not to teach these in schools and colleges. We need to develop a national language, but not at the dire expense of the regional languages. In a socialist economic and political context, the development of ethnic languages would not be inimical to national unity and consciousness. It is only in a competitive capitalist set-up that the warring interests exploit ethnic and regional language differences to the detriment of the common cause of the peasantry and the workers. That a study of our own languages is important for a meaningful self-image is increasingly being realized. At a recent conference on the study of Ghanaian languages at the University of Ghana, D. G. Ansare told the delegates:

> We have invited you here to share with you some of our needs. One of these is the need to realize that the systematic and careful study of our indigenous languages is a prerequisite to the better knowledge of ourselves, our way of life, our ideals of the beautiful, the true, the good and the holy. It is also an indirect aid in our performance in other languages, including English.[25]

Increased study of African languages will inevitably make more Africans want to write in their mother tongues and thus open new avenues for our creative imagination.

Schools of drama and music should be set up in African universities and other centres of learning, not as mere focuses for the academic study of African music and drama, but as nerve-centres for experiments in new forms and structures. Orchestras and drama companies resident at the schools and universities must go out to the villages and urban areas. The University should also be accessible to regional music and drama groups, to ensure a healthy mutual exchange of ideas and skills.

Most African universities and schools have departments of Fine Art where students go to learn sculpture, drawing and design. But apart from the approach to art in most such departments, which are run and organized as part of a Western mainstream, our very attitudes to art and to our artists have driven the artist to withdraw into himself, or into resignation. In terms of living, we have driven him to be dependent on the tourist. Often our artists paint or sculpt with one eye on these patrons. This ought to change. There must be a way of drawing our artists into the collective mainstream of the community. First, the academic criteria for entering a school of fine art should be removed or radically modified to make it possible for village artists to use the facilities. Even the selection of teachers should not be made on mere academic qualifications. After all, the African sculptors who have had such great influence on modern art were not trained in Western academic institutions. They moulded from a need arising out of the total religious involvement with the community. If a radical approach to art centres were adopted, we would be able to tap the artistic resources and skills in the country as a whole. And we must set up national galleries to collect any available traditional sculpture and crafts and to prevent the best of our contemporary output from going to other countries. Ideally, our social and economic life should be so organized that each village and each section of our cities is an art centre, a music centre, a drama centre. This would have the further advantage of rescuing our artists from their present dependence on the patronage of the tourist or outsider.

The above suggestions indicate how important the educational institutions are in the creation of a people's self-image. A radical re-structuring of our facilities should not be confined to the arts alone, but should extend to science, medicine, geography, in fact every aspect of learning, so that Africa becomes the centre:

In many discussions on the role of the university and indigenous culture, one is often confronted with a rather lazy question. How can one teach medicine, education, physics, agriculture, engineering, law and the rest of other university disciplines not associated with the humanities and bring out through their study and practice the African cultural values? I feel here that the answer must surely lie in two directions. The first and most important is in research. The second is in having the will and the courage to think. How many of our medical academics have, for instance, taken the trouble to study carefully and evaluate the importance of the wealth of curative psychiatry that the African medicine man uses in his practice of medicine. Does this not lie at the core of preventive and curative medicine in Africa? How many African educationists, for instance, have paused to read Mzee Kenyatta's education of a Kikuyu child in his book *Facing Mount Kenya* and have had the courage to think and evaluate the wealth of material based from our roots and cultural tradition that can help to build up a true philosophy of African education in all its exciting aspects of educating the full man? How many physicists have used the wealth of the African view of the cosmos to enrich the new western evaluated views and facts that are helped by advanced technology. Surely, it is not from wonder that man seeks truth. The magic wonder is an expression of a people's soul.[26]

The universities and our schools should go to the countryside; there must be total involvement with the creative struggle of the peasants and workers. The present dangerous, unhealthy gap between intellectual and practical labour, between the rural and urban centres, would be bridged. The centres of learning, the villages, the towns, would all be part of the blood stream revitalizing the whole body.

I believe that all these activities, important as they are, would be meaningless unless seen in the context of the kind of society we want. Our activities should not be aimed at enhancing reactionary traditionalism, irrelevant tribal solidarity, or élitism. After all, traditional tribal or ethnic unities are irrelevant and reactionary now that the economic bases on which they rested have been removed. In an interview with the Cuban revolutionary magazine *Tricontinental*, the leader of the Liberation Movement in Guinea and Cape Verde, Mr Amilcar Cabral, tackled this question as far as it affected his guerrilla forces against Portuguese colonialism:

> We believe that when the colonialists arrived in Africa the tribal structure was already in a state of disintegration due to the evolution of the economy and historical events on the African scene. Today it cannot be said that Africa is tribal. Africa still has remnants of tribalism, in particular as far as the mentality of the people is concerned, but not in the economic structure itself. Moreover, if colonialism, through its action, did anything positive at all, it was precisely to destroy a large part of the existing remnants of tribalism in certain parts of the country.[27]

We want to create a revolutionary culture which is not narrowly confined by the limitations of tribal traditions or national boundaries but looks outward to Pan-Africa and the Third World, and the needs of man. The national, the Pan-African, and the Third World awareness must be transformed into a socialist programme, or be doomed to sterility and death.

Having decided on this, we can then utilize all the resources at our disposal – radio, television, film, schools, universities, youth movements, farmers' co-operatives – to create such a society. (The film, especially, has great possibilities in Africa, where many people are still illiterate. But the film industry in Africa is practically non-existent.) In this way we shall find new strength and a new dynamic. Talking to teachers at Dar es Salaam earlier this year, Julius Nyerere urged them to teach to produce strength in the context of the revolutionary aims of the Arusha Declaration:

> Otherwise you will teach to produce clerks as the colonialists did. You will not be teaching fighters but a bunch of slaves or semi-slaves. Get your pupils out of the colonial mentality. You have to produce tough people; stubborn youths – who can do something – not hopeless youths.[28]

Any true national culture which can produce healthy 'stubborn youths', a culture that nurtures a society based on co-operation and not ruthless exploitation, ruthless grab-and-take, a culture that is born of a people's collective labour, such a culture will be best placed to contribute something truly positive and original to the modern world.

REFERENCES

1 Originally written in June 1969 as a background paper to the 1969 UNESCO conference on cultural policy in Africa in Dakar, but now considerably altered. The views expressed are personal and do not necessarily reflect those of the sponsors.

2 Melville J. Herskovits: *The Human Factor in Changing Africa* (New York, 1962) p. 3.

3 B. A. Ogot: *History of the Southern Luo* Vol. 1 (EAPH, Nairobi 1967) p. 3.

4 M. Fortes & E. E. Evans-Pritchard: *African Political Systems* (Oxford University Press, 1940), p. 5.

5 K. Onwuka Dike: *Trade and Politics in the Niger Delta* (Clarendon Press, Oxford, 1956) p. 44.

6 James Joyce: *A Portrait of the Artist as a Young Man* (Cape, London, 1956), Chap. V.

7 Matthew Arnold: *Culture and Anarchy* (Cambridge University Press, 1932) p. 48.

8 W. E. Abrahams: *The Mind of Africa* (Deutsch, London, 1967) p. 27.

9 Jomo Kenyatta: *Facing Mount Kenya* (Secker & Warburg, London, 1938) p. 317.

10 *The Tempest*, Act 1 Scene II.

11 *The Tempest*, Act 1, Scene II.

12 Isak Dinesen: *Shadows on the Grass* (John Murray, London, 1960) p. 13.

13 Shadows on the Grass p. 15.

14 Chinua Achebe: *Things Fall Apart* (Heinemann, London, 1958) p. 158.

15 Chinua Achebe: 'The African Writer as a Teacher', *Transition*.

16 Opening speech by Alioune Diop at the First World Conference of Negro Writers and Artists, Paris, 1956.

17 L. S. Senghor: Speech at the same conference.

18 Jomo Kenyatta: *Facing Mount Kenya* (Secker & Warburg, London, 1938).

19 Julius Nyerere: *Freedom and Socialism* (Oxford University Press, Nairobi, 1968) p. 235.

20 *Freedom and Socialism*, p. 233.

21 Sembène, Ousmane: *God's Bits of Wood* (Doubleday, New York, 1960 and Heinemann, London, 1970) p. 106.

22 Ngugi Henry Owuor-Anyumba, Taban Lo Liyong: 'On the Abolition of the English Department' in *Discussion Paper No. 1*. Faculty of Arts, Nairobi, 1968. (See Appendix).

23 Ngugi, Owuor-Anyumba, Taban Lo Liyong: op. cit.

24 Abiola Irele: 'The Teaching of Traditional African Literature' in *Proceedings of the Conference on the study of Ghanaian Languages* (ed. J. A. Birnie and D. G. Ansare).

25 D. G. Ansare: 'The need for a specific and comprehensive policy in the teaching of Ghanaian Languages', Birnie and Ansare. op. cit.

26 David Rubadiri: 'The University role in the development of East African culture', *East Africa's Heritage* (EAPH, Nairobi, 1966) p. 11.

27 Amilcar Cabral: 'Determined to Resist', *Tricontinental* No. 8, 1968.

28 Julius Nyerere: An unofficial translation by the Makerere Political Science Department, of a speech given to teachers at Dar es Salaam, January, 1969.

Kenya: The Two Rifts[1]

▼▼▼▼▼▼▼▼▼▼▼▼▼▼▼▼▼▼▼▼▼▼▼▼▼▼▼▼▼▼▼▼▼▼

I was born and grew up in Kenya. It is a land of hills and valleys; sunshine and rain; dry sand in the north and snow on the mountains; black and white races and a multiplicity of tribes. I have at times looked to the hills and ridges of Central Province and have remembered the Psalm of David:

I will lift up mine eyes unto the hills, from whence cometh my help.
My help cometh from the Lord, which made heaven and earth.

The Agikuyu believed that the Lord on High lived in the mountains, his chief dwelling place being Kirinyaga (Mt Kenya).

But the contrasts that make the worth and beauty of the land are at the same time the basis of conflicts. Contrasts and conflicts; that fairly summarizes the Kenya situation. Kenyatta saw this many years ago when he described Kenya as a land of conflicts. Then he must have been thinking about the tensions between the three main racial groups – Asian, African, and European. For these tensions form the major part of Kenya's history during the last sixty years.

The tensions have found expression at the political level. The African has always fought for a better political and economic position in his own country. The Asian has always struggled to achieve political parity with the European. And the European has all the time tried to preserve and perpetuate his dominant political and economic position at the top of the pyramid. Up to 1920, the battle was between the Asian and the European, the subject of the struggle being representation in the Legislative Council, in which the Asian wanted equal representation. He argued that he was a British subject, and was an immigrant just as much as the European. He also argued that he had contributed much to the country's social and economic growth. On the basis of output, had he not, then, a right to political equality? The Asian lost the battle. Then the African came on the scene. He began to organize himself into political parties. Leaders came from among the 'mission boys' who had been educated at the mission schools. Let us be clear about this: the African's grievances did not just begin in 1920 – in fact they had always been there even before 1900. But he had no way of voicing his complaints and dissatisfaction except through sporadic acts of violence and sabotage. With the emergence of people who could talk the white man's language, the African voice became louder and louder. The African was now a factor in the struggle. The other races were aware of this. The battle then became three-cornered.

It is a credit to the African that he has always sought for constitutional and 'legitimate' means of righting the position. Discussion and compromise had always been the African way of settling disputes. But this was denied to him. Until recently, political parties were not given a chance to work normally. The colonial government, while aware of their existence, shut its ears to their urgent voices. Frustration mounted on frustration. Then one day came the crisis. The Mau Mau War was and will remain a bitter lesson for Kenya.

With the 1960 and 1962 Lancaster House agreements the African was on the way to victory. A large section of the Asian and European populations became reconciled to the independence of Kenya under African rule.

But, and this is the point, the conflicts will continue. For the political tensions patterned on race have perpetuated three ways of life that have apparently no meeting ground. The three races have never had a culture contact. They have never really met. They have never known each other, so how do they hope to understand one another?

They must remain strangers in the same land. They must remain sharply divided by a vertical rift. Few have been adventurous and courageous enough to cross the rift and see what is on the other side. The African, and especially the Asian and the European, had each lived in his racial shell.

Even among the Africans, this curse of separate development is seen in tribal conflicts and suspicions, best symbolized by the KANU (Kenya African National Union) and KADU (Kenya African Democratic Union) line-up. Some leaders of KADU were heard to speak of the partition of Kenya into its tribal constituents – a contradiction of what is implied by the name of the party.

In Kenya then, there is really no concept of a nation. One is always a Kikuyu, a Luo, a Nandi, an Asian or a European. I think this diminishes our strength and creative power. To live on the level of race or tribe is to be less than whole. In order to live, a chick has to break the shell shutting it out from the light. Man too must break the shell and be free. Political freedom from foreign rule, essential as it is, is not *the* freedom. One freedom is essential. This is the freedom for man to develop into his full potential. He cannot do this as long as he is enslaved by certain shackles.

Two of these are racism and tribalism. To look from the tribe to a wider concept of human association is to be progressive. When this begins to happen, a Kenya nation will be born. It will be an association, not of different tribal entities, but of individuals, free to journey to those heights of which they are capable. Nationalism, by breaking some tribal shells, will be a help. But nationalism should not in turn become another shackle. Nor should it be the end. The end should be man ultimately freed from fear, suspicion and parochial attitudes: free to develop and realize his full creative potential.

Kenya is potentially a great country. The contrasts that are the basis of conflicts could be the basis of strength, beauty and progress. The different springs in every tribe and race can and should be channelled to flow together in a national stream from which all may draw. In the past, the virtues and energies to be found in different peoples have been used for the political struggle in a society vertically divided into tribal and racial pillars. These good qualities should now be harmonized to work for a national ideal.

In the long run, however, tribalism and even racialism will die. Tribalism cannot withstand for long the rising tide of African nationalism and commercial individualism. And so one looks hopefully to a time in the near future when this vertical rift will vanish. There will then be no conflicting pillars in the same society.

But Kenya, like many other countries in Africa, is faced with another rift: a horizontal rift dividing the élite from the mass of the people. In a sense this rift in society dividing the upper from the lower is a universal one, not solely confined to the emerging nations of Africa. It divides the rich from the poor, the educated from the uneducated. Disraeli saw this rift in nineteenth-century Britain and wrote about it in his novel *The Two Nations*.

The situation in the emerging countries is made urgent by the fact that the educated are very few and the great illiterate mass looks up to them for leadership and guidance. The educated, then, have not only political power but economic power as well. The educated have better economic opportunities than the uneducated. Will this class use their political power to entrench their economic position? Julius Nyerere has clearly seen such a possibility. He has warned against a society in which the gap between the 'few haves' and the 'mass of have-nots' is too wide. More than this, he has pointed out the danger of the educated class assuming the position formerly held by Europeans. This could divide the nation under formation. This educated few could easily monopolize not only the political and economic power but culture as well. A culture which is the preserve of the top few is not a national culture. It is not a national stream from which all may draw.

There is no clear-cut solution to the problem of these rifts. Any solution must lie with the different individuals that make up Kenya society. The traditional African concept of *the* community should not be forgotten in our rush for western culture and political institutions, which some regard as the ready-made solution to our problems. In the African way, the community serves the individual. And the individual finds the fullest development of his personality when he is working in and for the community as a whole. Land, food and wealth is for the community. In this community, culture belongs to all. For the rich and poor, the foolish and the wise are all free to participate in the national life of the community in all its manifestations. Perhaps this is what some have meant when they talk of African socialism. If so, it is a worthy ideal.

I do not propose a solution to such a vast problem. I have said that the solution lies with the people of Kenya. One thing however is necessary in any attempt to eradicate these rifts. People must have that attitude of mind that is not only aware of the problems, but desires a solution. For Kenya a national culture embracing all can be developed. It is what earlier on I called a national ideal, for which in the past the different peoples have not looked. But if the people of Kenya can lift up their eyes unto the hills, and especially to Mt Kenya, and stretch their wings ready to fly to freedom and life, the shells will break. They will be free.

A dream? One has only to go to Kenya to know. All the people love her soil dearly. This is our common ground. Perhaps the soil, which in the traditional view was always seen as a source of creative life and fertility, will unite them. In this lies the hope of Kenya.

REFERENCES

1 First appeared in *The New African*, Vol. 1, No. 9, September 1962.

Mau Mau, Violence and Culture[1]

▼▼▼▼▼▼▼▼▼▼▼▼▼▼▼▼▼▼▼▼▼▼▼▼▼▼▼▼▼▼▼▼▼▼

The conflicts in the land of Kenya, at their most marked in the relationship between the African and the European, have operated on three planes: political, economic, and cultural. The white settler came early in the century and he immediately controlled the heart of the economy by appropriating the best part of the land to himself. Alienation of land, after all, was then the declared British colonial policy for the region which later became Kenya. The settler was told that this would be a white man's country, and he was able to use his political power to consolidate his economic position. He forced black men into labour gangs, working for him in the 'White Highlands'. He rationalized this exploitation of African land and labour by claiming he was civilizing a primitive people. The government and the missionary aided the settler in this belief: after all, the three were an integral product or representative of the same social force: capitalism. That the African was a child was a basic premise: if the African wanted a share in the government, he was told that he had yet to grow. He had to acquire the ways and style of life of the white man – through the slow process of watching and imitating from a distance. The white settler, then, effectively exploited differences in culture to keep the reins of political and economic power out of the black man's hands.

It will therefore be seen that in the Kenyan scene of the last sixty years you cannot separate economics and culture from politics. The three are interwoven. A cultural assertion was an integral part of the political and economic struggle.

Only in terms of all these different and yet closely interrelated planes of conflict can the Mau Mau revolution of 1952 be understood. To single out one of them, especially the cultural, and work it into an elaborate explanation of this great political revolt is a gross oversimplification. And yet this is what nearly all European writers on Mau Mau have done.[2] Fred Majdalany, in his book *State of Emergency*, is no different. He sees Mau

Mau as being the result of the failure of a primitive culture to withstand the impact of a superior one. He writes:

> It [the Mau Mau Emergency] could be said to have begun when the first European settlers came to the country and in good faith tried to impose their own ways and their idea of civilisation on a group of primitive peoples still living in something akin to the stone age.

Those who have bothered to study the social and political structure of the Agikuyu, as of most African people, will at once recognize the lie in the words 'primitive' and 'akin to stone age' to describe their culture. To writers like Majdalany, any 'culture' which is not recognizably western must of course be primitive.

The book is divided into two parts; the period before 1952 and then the period of the Emergency. In his account of the earlier history, the author borrows heavily from Corfield, a man who had been commissioned to vindicate the Kenya Colonial Government in its ruthless suppression of a nationalist struggle.

Fred Majdalany fails to see that the economic conflict was at the heart of the matter. The alienated (polite word for stolen) land has always been the key to Kenya's problem, as indeed it is to all the settler colonies of Central and South Africa. But how could he understand this when, with the complacency of a self-styled expert on early land alienation, he can utter half-truths with such ease?

> You could walk for miles and miles through the deserted spaces without seeing a human soul.

So could you in the so-called White Highlands, so massive was the land given to people like Delamere and Grogan! And in another place:

> It was only later, when settler-African relationship was becoming a problem, that the myth was created that the settlers had stolen the best land . . .

Obviously he had not consulted even some of the documented evidence. He thinks that there was no land ownership among the Agikuyu. Could he not at least have read Kenyatta's book *Facing Mount Kenya*? Corfield and the conversation he had with settlers were enough for this author.

The section on the Gikuyu is a repetition of the old stereotyped attitudes, obviously gained from the same conversations. Yet, for 'The Full Story of Mau Mau', the book's sub-title, Mr Majdalany consulted only the Colonial Office, the Kenya government officials, members of the administration at the time of the Emergency, the generals and the chiefs – who were all anti-Mau Mau. Not once did he try to get the picture from the other side. As a result the book is full of stale generalizations. He mixes myth with some semblance of liberal objectivity.

His account of the Emergency period is no better. Again it is clouded with the popular image of the Mau Mau as something purely and simply evil, atavistic and completely unrelated to the mainstream of African nationalism or any decent political sentiments. To most Africans, Mau Mau in fact was a heroic and glorious aspect of that mainstream. The basic objectives of Mau Mau revolutionaries were to drive out the Europeans, seize the government, and give back to the Kenya peasants their stolen lands and property. It is not surprising that it was anti-European and anti-Christian. What else did Majdalany expect? That the oppressed would go about singing hymns of praise to the people who had oppressed and exploited them for over sixty years? Every revolutionary movement is anti-the people who run and perpetuate an oppressive exploiting system, is anti- the cultural and religious values and assumptions which are used to rationalize that oppression and exploitation.

Majdalany is horrified by the savage acts of Mau Mau. These fall into two categories: oathing and the actual violence. The oath was not a simple avowal to attend a Sunday afternoon picnic; it was a commitment to sabotage the colonial machine and to kill if necessary. The oath, especially in its second and third rounds, was tough and strong: to have taken it was a measure of one's total commitment to the group and to the African cause. This was not the first time in history that a secret society has had to participate in strong communal rites that break ordinary social taboos as an act of group solidarity and as a test of their complete dedication to the cause of liberation. Even worthless WASPish fraternal societies in America, or Freemasons in Europe, participate in unusual types of oaths. In Shakespeare's *Antony and Cleopatra*, Octavius cites Anthony's willingness to eat revolting bestial food as a measure of his soldierly qualities and dedication. The point is not whether oaths are 'bestial' or not, but the nature of the particular historical circumstances that make them necessary and the cause they serve.

The same applies to violence. Violence in order to change an intolerable, unjust social order is not savagery: it purifies man. Violence to protect and preserve an unjust, oppressive social order is criminal, and diminishes man. To gloat in the latter form of violence, as Ian Henderson does in his

The Hunt for Dedan Kimathi, is revolting. In Kenya, then, we were confronted with two forms of violence. The British perpetrated violence on the African people for fifty years. In 1952, once the political leaders were arrested and detained, the colonial régime intensified its acts of indiscriminate terrorism, thereby forcing many peasants and workers to take to the forests. For about four years, these people, with little experience of guerrilla warfare, without help from any outside powers, organized themselves and courageously resisted the British military forces. It is true that after the capture of Dedan Kimathi the men became disorganized, became desperate and tended to rely more and more on the 'advice of witchdoctors' instead of a clear analysis and understanding of the forces against them. The disorganized end of Mau Mau should not be confused with its heroic beginnings and its four years of spectacular resistance to the enemy forces. Mau Mau violence was anti-injustice; white violence was to thwart the cause of justice. Should we equate the two forms? Even if we take 'savage' act for 'savage' act, can the civilized whites be exonerated? Majdalany doggedly refuses to tell the full story of several crucial incidents. He recounts what is generally called the Lari massacre in colonial records, but does not add that many of the killed were collaborators with the enemy forces and hence traitors to the African cause: that many innocent men and women were afterwards led to the forest and summarily executed by the government forces. I know six who were taken from my village, which was miles from Lari. The relatives of the six murdered people tried to take the case to the courts, but this never came to anything. Such was the nature of colonial justice in Kenya, even before this period of war.

And the story of those who were taken to detention camps – without trials? On this subject the author conveniently remains quiet. An incident like that of the Hola, which aroused the ordinary British people to a protest, is not even mentioned.

Things have now changed in Kenya. Jomo Kenyatta, who in this book is dismissed as an agitator, is now the Prime Minister.[3] Everywhere in the country he is being called the saviour. He led his party, the Kenya African National Union, to an emphatic victory, defeating a combination of his rival parties aided by the settler community, with more than forty seats in the House of Representatives. He got support from the peasant masses and urban workers because he was a symbol of their deepest aspirations. To have imprisoned him was futile, because he was himself only a symbol of social forces which could never be finally put down by the gun.

It is in the light of such post-emergency happenings that I think somebody with intellectual honesty should write the full history of Mau Mau as a cultural, political and economic expression of the aspirations of the African peasant masses, putting it in its revolutionary context.

REFERENCES

1 A review of *A State of Emergency: The Full Story of Mau Mau* by Fred Madjalany. (Houghton Mifflin, Boston, 1963). The review was written in 1963.

2 Since 1963, there have been some 'good' books on Mau Mau, the most notable being: Donald L. Barrett and Karari Njama: *Mau Mau from Within* (MacGibbon & Kee, London, 1966); Carl G. Rosberg and John Nottingham: *The Myth of Mau Mau* (EAPH, Nairobi. First published in 1966 in USA for Stanford University); J. M. Kariuki: *Mau Mau Detainee* (OUP, London, 1963).

3 Now (1972) President of the Republic of Kenya.

Church, Culture and Politics[1]

▼▼▼▼▼▼▼▼▼▼▼▼▼▼▼▼▼▼▼▼▼▼▼▼▼▼▼

I feel slightly uneasy standing before this great Assembly of the Presbyterian Church of East Africa. I am not a man of the Church. I am not even a Christian. I make that confession because I don't want to be misunderstood. I don't want to be accused of hypocrisy: for some will ask, 'How can you, a non-believer, dare to talk about the role of the Church in Africa today?'

I am a writer. Some have even called me a religious writer. I write about people: I am interested in their hidden lives; their fears and hopes, their loves and hates, and how the very tension in their hearts affects their daily contact with other men: how, in other words, the emotional stream of the man within interacts with the social reality.

I believe that the Christian faith (or religious faith in general) is concerned with the inner lives of the people. That is why I need not apologize for being here today. I want to share with you my fears and hopes.

But there is another reason. As a Kenyan African I cannot escape from the Church. Its influence is all around me. For Kenya perhaps more than other parts of Africa has gone through certain difficult periods in her history, which have been a result of the contradiction inherent in colonialism and its religious ally, the Christian Church.

I say contradiction because Christianity, whose basic doctrine was love and equality between men, was an integral part of that social force – colonialism – which in Kenya was built on the inequality and hatred between men and the consequent subjugation of the black race by the white race.

The coming of Christianity also set in motion a process of social change, involving rapid disintegration of the tribal set-up and the frame-work of social norms and values by which people had formerly ordered their lives and their relationship to others. This was especially true of Central Province, where the Church of Scotland Mission, which has a highly strict puritan tradition, could not separate the strictly Christian dogma or doctrine from the European scale of values, and from European customs. The evidence that you were saved was not whether you were a believer in and follower of Christ, and accepted all men as equal: the measure of your

Christian love and charity was in preserving the outer signs and symbols of a European way of life; whether you dressed as Europeans did, whether you had acquired European good manners, liked European hymns and tunes, and of course whether you had refused to have your daughter circumcised.

Thus acceptance of the Christian Church meant the outright rejection of all the African customs. It meant rejection of those values and rituals that held us together: it meant adopting what in effect was a debased European middle-class mode of living and behaviour. The European missionary had attacked the primitive rites of our people, had condemned our beautiful African dances, the images of our gods, recoiling from their suggestion of satanic sensuality. The early African convert did the same, often with even greater zeal, for he had to prove how Christian he was through this rejection of his past and roots.

So that in Kenya, while the European settler robbed people of their land and the products of their sweat, the missionary robbed people of their soul. Thus was the African body and soul bartered for thirty pieces of silver and the promise of a European heaven.

Education was not an adequate answer to the hungry soul of the African masses because it emphasized the same Christian values that had refused to condemn (in fact helped) the exploitation of the African body and mind by the European colonizer. The first education given was merely to enable converts to read the Bible, so that they could carry out simple duties as assistants to the missionaries. As education later came to be the ladder to better jobs and money and to a higher standard of living, albeit in the image of the European mode of life, the Christian-educated African became even more removed from his ancestral shrines and roots. The conflict between the Kenya people and the missionary churches, the subsequent setting up of African independent churches, and the religious aspects of the Mau Mau liberation movement, were direct results of the culture conflict initiated by the missionary holy zeal. The breakaway churches all over Kenya tried to create a form of worship and evolve an education more in tune and harmony with peoples' hopes, incorporating as some did the best in our traditional approach to God and the Universe. They wanted, in the words of Professor Alan Ogot and the Reverend F. B. Welbourn, to build a place to feel at home.

The Church in Kenya today is a creation of the European missionaries. And we have said that the missionaries were part of that momentous upheaval in our history – the coming of colonialism. Or rather, missionaries, settlers and administrators were agents of European imperialism. It has been said with truth that the trader and the settler followed the skirts and shirt-cuffs of the missionary. In some places in Africa political power was established at the request and instigation of the missionaries of the imperialist country. Livingstone and Cecil Rhodes, Dr Arthur and Lord Delamere, were these not part of that movement that came into such a fatal collision with our way of life and identity?

Even our people came to see the Church and the settler community as one. The Gikuyu saying 'Gutiri Muthungu na Mubia' (i.e., there is no difference between the European and the missionary priest) is a good example of this identification of the missionary with the settler.

Some of the missionaries, perhaps without knowing it and with the best intentions, encouraged this. The fight between the Catholics and Protestants for the control of the court of Mutesa of Buganda was in fact a struggle between French capitalism and British capitalism for the control of Uganda. The Protestants were helped by British mercenaries like Lugard and Stanley. Thus Africans in Uganda became the sport of European mercenary greed, under the guise of Christianity and work for God. In reading these accounts one is impressed by the desire of the missionaries not to bring light to the African souls, but to wrest political power from the then Kabaka as a means of controlling the country and bringing it within the orbit of influence of their particular nations.

Often missionaries became landowners and kept cattle on the stolen lands, and these flourished very well – under African labour. This on top of similar alienation of land by settlers made people see religion as something to blind the black races with while the white race stole peoples' national property. You know the popular story among our people: that the Mubia told people to shut their eyes in prayer, and when later they opened their eyes, the land was taken. And then, so the story goes, the Mubia told them not to worry about those worldly things which could be eaten by moth; and they sang: *Thĩ ĩno ti yakwa ndĩ mwĩhĩtũkĩri* ('this world is not my home, I am only a pilgrim').

But apart from the doctrine that poverty and the poor were blessed and would get their reward in heaven, the missionary preached the need to obey the powers that be. The saying 'render unto Caesar things that are Caesar's' was held up to the African church-goers and schoolchildren. No matter how morally corrupt Caesar was, the African Christian was told to obey him. In this case Caesar was the colonial power. To tell the African that politics and political agitation was a dirty game and inconsistent with the Christian faith was a very easy step.

Thus it came to pass that the Church became the greatest opponent of the African struggle for freedom. The Church opposed Mau Mau, but never the colonial Caesar. It saw the Mau Mau liberation movement as being savage and anti-Christian: it did not see the policies of the colonial powers, in depriving people of their land, in making them work for a pittance, in depriving them of legal rights, in having them beaten and mistreated by the Delameres and the Grogans, as the exact opposite of all the Church was supposed to stand for. The Church appeared to say: the white Caesar can do no wrong; white is good, while black is bad and wrong. The Church, instead of fighting against the real colonial anti-Christ, vigorously fought against those who were prepared to lose their lives that many might live.

Yet Christ himself had always championed the cause of the Jewish masses against both the Pharisees (equivalent to our privileged bourgeoisie) and the Roman colonialists: he was in any case crucified on the orders of the Roman conquerors. One could say that if Christ had lived in Kenya in 1952, or in South Africa or Rhodesia today, he would have been crucified as a Mau Mau terrorist, or a Communist.

The Church then refused to speak up when oppressive measures were taken by the colonial Caesar, but spoke against people who rose up in arms against oppression. In face of a colour bar and discrimination against the black race the Church only preached about heaven and the life to come.

Moreover, the very reactionary political views of some missionaries has left a bad legacy among some African church leaders, who still tend to view religious life as that of a hermit divorced from the daily cry of the masses for a more effective control of their national economy.

I am stressing these things of our colonial religious inheritance because if the Church is to mean anything then it must be a meaningful champion of the needs of all the workers and peasants of this country. It must adapt itself in form and in content to provide a true spiritual anchor in the continuing struggle of the masses in today's Africa.

So what could be the role of the Church today?

Again forgive me if I digress a little and look at the role of the Church in the past. Again I want to stress that I am talking of the Church as a corporate body, an institution, and not of the individual holders of the faith.

In Europe, the churches and their leaders were always in alliance with the ruling classes. The Church always changed its posture to conform to or rationalize the exploitation of the masses by the ruling classes, even to the point, in the Catholic Church, where people were told how to vote.

The Church has, in the past, justified slavery because the ruling classes of Europe needed slavery and the slave trade. Millions of black people were transported to America and the West Indies and sold with the knowledge and tacit approval of the Church. And as the slaves moaned and died of beating, lack of air, and starvation, one of the slave-masters had time to compose the touching hymn 'How sweet the name of Jesus sounds in a believer's ear'. In Latin America some religious leaders who have had the courage as individuals to speak up against the rich landowners and the corrupt military régimes have often been thrown out of the Church.

In South Africa (despite the courage of a few individual Christians like Father Huddleston) the Church tacitly accepts Apartheid, and would oppose violence to overthrow this evil régime, this great white anti-Christ.

In America, Billy Graham, who has been responsible for the mass conversion of many people, and often comes to Africa, to convert Africans to his Christ, was a great friend of ex-President Johnson and refused, when asked to, to condemn American continued massacre of the Vietnamese people. In fact he supported the American occupation of Vietnam.

But even the Church in the Western world is undergoing much upheaval because it has become out of date through its continued alliance with the ruling class and industrial magnates. The churches no longer represent the aspirations and beliefs of the people, and their circle of loyal followers is dwindling because their teaching and practices do not represent the genuine struggle of the working masses.

Can the Church in Africa be different?

I have talked of the Church's role in the past in the area of culture and of social involvement. If the Church in the past has been the greatest cause of the misshaping of African souls and cultural alienation, it must, today, work for cultural integration. It must go back to the roots of the broken African civilization: it must examine the traditional African forms of marriage, traditional African forms of sacrifice. Why were these things meaningful and wholesome to the traditional African community? What was the secret of Mundu Mugo, of the rainmaker? What of the mountains, the moon, the trees, Mugumo for instance? What of the drums and dances and even ceremonial drinking and forms of oath-taking? Can the core of Christian faith find anchor in some of these symbols, or must it be for ever clothed in the joyless drab and dry European middle-class culture? Must our priests continue to wear the robes they now wear? Build the kind of Churches they now build? Cut the cakes they cut at white wedding ceremonies? Why is cutting a cake and giving a ring a more Christian ceremony than eating Njahi or slaughtering goats and sprinkling beer to our ancestors? Why is wine at Holy Communion more clean and Christian than Njohi? These are not idle questions: for the symbols with which we choose to identify ourselves are important in expressing the values held by a community.

But ultimately the African Church's greatest danger is in its area of social involvement. After independence an African middle-class was born: this class is busy grabbing and amassing land and business concerns at the expense of the peasant and working masses. I would refer you to a quotation in 'Who Controls Kenya's Industry?', the Report of a Working Party set up under the auspices of the National Christian Council of Kenya:

> There is a clear class division in Kenya's society – which is based on the share of economic wealth of the nation. Kenya society provides a very good example of haves and the have-nots.

Will the Church, as has happened in Europe and Latin America, form an alliance with this bureaucratic commercial middle-class élite, the members of which in any case act as agents of foreign capitalism? Can the Church as a body reject the exploitation of the masses by a few who because of the benefits of education and control of social institutions are in a position to amass so much wealth? Will the Church reject capitalism, which has been found wasteful and inhuman?

I believe the Church could return to (or learn lessons from) the primitive communism of the early Christian Church of Peter and also the communalism of the traditional African society. With this, and working in alliance with the socialist aspirations of the African masses, we might build a new society to create a new man freed from greed and competitive hatred, and ready to realize his full potential in humble co-operation with other men in a just socialist society. Remember that Book of Revelation: 'I saw a new heaven and a new earth' . . . Yes, but the cry of the psalmist in the Old Testament is more apt to our situation: 'How shall we sing the Lord's song in a strange land?' I believe that Christians, together with members of other organizations which avow humanism, could help in the struggle to move away from the strange land of capitalism, neo-colonialism and western middle-class culture. For this we may very well need to destroy the old temple to build a new, different one.

REFERENCES

1 Speech made at the Fifth General Assembly of the Presbyterian Church of East Africa at Nairobi: 12 March 1970.

Part Two: Writers in Africa

Part Two WORK RATE

The Writer and His Past[1]

I want to talk about the past as a way of talking about the present. It was Aristotle who wrote that the distinction between the historian and the poet was that one describes the thing that has been, and the other a kind of thing that might be. Aristotle was in part talking of history and poetry as a method of dealing with reality, and concluded that 'poetry is something more philosophic and of graver import than history, since the statements are of the nature of universals whereas those of history are singular.'

Here I want to argue that what has been – the evolution of human culture through the ages, society in motion through time and space – is of grave import to the poet and the novelist. For what has been, especially for the vast majority of submerged, exploited masses in Africa, Asia and Black America, is intimately bound up with what might be: our vision of the future, of diverse possibilities of life and human potential, has roots in our experience of the past. In the words of T. S. Eliot:

> Time present and time past
> Are both perhaps present in time future,
> And time future contained in time past.

The novelist is haunted by a sense of the past. His work is often an attempt to come to terms with 'the thing that has been', a struggle, as it were, to sensitively register his encounter with history, his people's history.

And the novelist, at his best, must feel himself heir to a continuous tradition. He must feel himself, as I think Tolstoy did in *War and Peace* or Sholokov in *And Quiet Flows the Don*, swimming, struggling, defining himself, in the mainstream of his people's historical drama. At the same time, he must be able to stand aside and merely contemplate the currents. He must do both: simultaneously swim, struggle and also watch, on the shore.

But occasionally, in the process, he feels that his feet are unsteady, that he has been uprooted, that he is not heir to a continuous culture. Where do I stand in the mainstream? he asks. Has there been a mainstream, anyway?

He becomes nervous; he feels himself alienated; he is, but may not know it, one of those twentieth-century strangers in a world they have created, through sweat and blood, but which they cannot call their own. He frantically looks around and asks: where is my past, where is my history?

The West Indian novelist is a case in point. In his book *The Pleasures of Exile* George Lamming has bitterly complained that the West Indian has been severed from his roots, and hence has embraced colonialism as the very base and structure of his cultural awareness:

What the West Indian shares with the African is a common political predicament: a predicament which we call colonial; but the word colonial has a deeper meaning for the West Indian than it has for the African. The African, in spite of his modernity, has never been wholly severed from the cradle of a continuous culture.[2]

The West Indian novel in English is in part preoccupied with a general quest for roots. Beneath most West Indian fictional characters there lurks a sense of exile. Alienation, individual and communal, is the one unifying theme in the West Indian novel. Two examples will do. In *An Absence of Ruins*, a novel by Orlando Patterson, the main character is always conscious of standing 'outside of race, outside of history, outside of any value'. Another character in the same novel is made to say:

We are all Jews lost in the wilderness, brother, and we are all black men, according to the Word. And the Word, which is the Truth, say unto I: In this world, in this life, every man is a Jew searching for his Zion; every man is a black man lost in a white world of grief.[3]

Admittedly, Patterson makes his characters too conscious of their predicaments and alienation. Nevertheless, these features haunt one's memory because one feels they are real problems for all colonial middle classes who cannot see their link with the masses and their past. The awareness of vacuum, of chaos, of emptiness as the very condition of a colonial middle class links *An Absence of Ruins* to V. S. Naipaul's novel *The Mimic Men*. Singh, the hero, is a failed politician who finds himself in exile in London. The exploration of his predicament is bound up with Naipaul's rather cynical glance at the breaking up of colonial empires, and the operation of political power:

The career of the colonial politician is short and ends brutally. We lack order. Above all, we lack power, and we do not understand that we lack power.[4]

His fear of disorder is brilliantly symbolized in his obsessional fears that his house, in the West Indies, would collapse.

> I developed the fear that our old timber house was unsafe. It was not uncommon in our city for houses to tumble down; during the rainy season our newspapers were full of such tragedies. I began to look for these reports, and every report added to my fear. As soon as I lay down on my bed, my heart beat faster, and I mistook its throbbing for the shaking of the house. At times my head swam; I felt my bed tilt and I held on in a cold sweat until the disturbance passed.[5]

Well, a house built on sand is likely to fall. And that's what we are talking about. What is my past, what is my history, so necessary for my communal as well as for my individual self-image? asks the writer.

Many African writers would agree with George Lamming that the African has not been completely severed from his roots. In the Preface to his play *The Survivors*, Dr Gideon Were of Kenya makes an interesting comment on European colonization:

> The whole irony of the European occupation is that its effect on the basic social values and customs of the African peoples was virtually negligible. It is as if the Europeans had stopped over in the country for only a couple of years or so.[6]

Dr Were oversimplifies the effect of European occupation. For although the African's progress, unlike that of his West Indian counterpart, has not been through what Eric Williams calls 'the broiling sun of the sugar, tobacco and cotton plantations', the African, through his colonial education, found his image of the past distorted. His colonial middle-class education and brainwashing told him that he had no history. The black man did not really exist, had slept in the dark continent until the Livingstones and the Stanleys woke him into history through a mixture of piety and violence, the Bible and the gun.

Note that Prospero's arrogance had a respectable intellectual basis. Some of the best minds of Europe and the West generally have abetted this grand deception about the black man's place in human history. Listen to Hegel:

> Africa proper, as far as history goes back, has remained for all purposes of connection with the rest of the world – shut up; it is the Gold-Land compressed within itself – the land of childhood, which lying beyond the days of self-conscious history, is enveloped in the dark mantle of the night.

The Negro as already observed exhibits the natural man in his completely wild and untamed state. We must lay aside all thought of reverence and morality – all that we call feeling – if we would comprehend him; there is nothing harmonious with humanity to be found in this type of character.

At this point we leave Africa never to mention it again. For it is no historical part of the world; it has no movement to exhibit. Historical movement in it – that is in its northern part – belongs to the Asiatic or European world . . .

What we understand by Africa, is the unhistorical under-developed spirit, still involved in the condition of nature . . .

The history of the world travels from East to West, for Europe is absolutely the end of history, Asia the beginning.[7]

We could mention others: H. G. Wells, who had no place for Africa in his amateurish history of the world, or more recently Hugh Trevor-Roper, the English historian, who despite all the evidence of modern archaeological, historical, and anthropological scholarship, thinks that Africa had only darkness to exhibit before the colonial era. Every oppressive system, from ancient Rome to modern America, has had its religious and intellectual apologists, whose aim is to show that the oppressed have no feet other than the props provided by the master.

Prospero also dabbled in creative magic. He tried to fashion Caliban in something like Hegel's negative image of Caliban's past. Prospero after all supposes he has discovered Caliban. So he puts him into fiction. The African character in Rider Haggard's novels is either a noble savage with gleaming white teeth and assegais, or else a sub-human crook waiting in the dark to harm the white adventurer. Often his good natives are seized with illogical terror and look up to the reassuring presence of the white protector. A relevant comparison is with the Western. Most cowboy films are based on the myth of a lone band of white men out-numbered by swarms of bloodthirsty Indians. Our cowboy who plays it cool eventually wins. Tarzan, still going strong in western comic strips, is a 'cowboy' in the African jungle. These myths, perpetuated in fiction by such writers as Robert Ruark, still pervade European and American television screens and have made nauseating films on Africa, like *Simba, Guns of Batasi, Africa Addio*, they are readily accepted and applauded by European audiences.

It might be argued that Rider Haggard, Robert Ruark, and the creators of Tarzan are special cases. But even in the novels of the so-called liberal writers, the African character remains fundamentally a child at the mercy of irrational forces. He has no vital relationship with his environment, with his past. He does not create; he is created. Elspeth Huxley, that liberal apologist for Kenya settlers, is a case in point. Her novel *The Red Strangers* deals with the encounter between the Gikuyu people and the new forces of imperialism. But the African characters, as Ezekiel Mphahlele has pointed out, act rather strangely when confronted by the white man. Their will to act melts away even without the kind of inner conflict which we would normally expect in any human being confronted with alien forces he cannot comprehend. Her good characters are those who live in stupid perpetual puzzlement about the ways of the white man. The rebels are nearly always thugs and crooks, whose motives in fighting for the rights of black people are highly suspect. 'The characters in *The Red Strangers*,' Ezekiel Mphahlele has written in *The African Image*, 'are very much like prehistoric man to whom so many things happened without stirring in him a will that he would impose on the scheme of things and deflect its course.'

The same can be said of the good Christian souls in Alan Paton's *Cry the Beloved Country*, who suffer without bitterness, and move through an oppressive régime without even being stirred to anger. Stephen Kumalo is a pathetic creature acted on by his environment – and he is always understanding and full of Christian forgiveness. *Cry the Beloved Country* was another *Uncle Tom's Cabin* – in Africa. The failure in imaginative comprehension of the African character in European fiction lies in the fact that the African is not seen in an active causal-effect relationship with a significant past. Kumalo has no god; he can only look to the merciful white man's god for deliverence.

What the African novelist has attempted to do is restore the African character to his history. The African novelist has turned his back on the Christian god and resumed the broken dialogue with the gods of his people. He has given back to the African character the will to act and change the scheme of things. Writers like Peter Abrahams and Chinua Achebe have paved the way.

Peter Abrahams despite his broken vision, broken, that is, because his realism in depicting the social conditions of workers in South Africa fortunately negates his romantic, sentimental vision of a society without colour, has tried to assert the African humanity in face of the Haggardian tradition and naked white racism. The traditional African society in *The Wild Conquest*, the story of the black-white encounter in the 'great' trek, is seen as a complex living organ: its doctors had a knowledge of psychology in the treatment of psychic disorders and disease. The Haggardian savage was thus turned into a modern psychiatrist. In *Mine Boy*, Xuma, the hero, asserts his humanity in the struggle against South African slavery and racist exploitation. Calling on other workers to come out on strike against the appalling working conditions in the South African mines, he shouts: 'We are men. It does not matter if our skins are black. We are not cattle to throw away our lives. We are men.' Chinua Achebe's characters, shaped by a different social climate, do not have to assert their humanity. This is assumed. They have a vital relationship with their social and economic landscape. We can see, and feel, how his characters, their world-view, their very aspirations, have been shaped by a particular environment in a particular historical phase. They live in history – yet are not mere cogs in the machine – because they (the Okonkwos and Ezeulus) are the makers of history. He has succeeded in giving human dignity to his characters, whether living in their traditional communal life or resisting European colonialism. Achebe in fact is very explicit about his intentions as a writer. He sees his task as helping his society to regain its belief in itself and to put away the complexes of the years of denigration and self-denigration. His four novels – *Things Fall Apart, Arrow of God, No Longer at Ease, A Man of the People* – are a brave and successful attempt to recreate the dynamic spirit of a living community.

In East Africa the novelists and poets are hearkening to Okot p'Bitek's poem, *Song of Lawino*.[8]

> Listen Ocol, my old friend
> The ways of your ancestors
> Are good,
> Their customs are solid
> And not hollow
> They are not thin, not easily breakable
> They cannot be blown away
> By the winds,
> Because their roots reach deep into the soil.

Lawino, the heroine of the poem, is only insisting on the primacy of her African world and her historical experience.

But the African writer was in danger of becoming too fascinated by the yesterday of his people and forgetting the present. Involved as he was in correcting his disfigured past, he forgot that his society was no longer peasant, with common ownership of means of production, with communal celebration of joy and victory, communal sharing of sorrow and bereavement; his society was no longer organized on egalitarian principles. Conflicts between the emergent élitist middle-class and the masses were developing, their seeds being in the colonial pattern of social and economic development. And when he woke up to his task he was not a little surprised that events in post-independence Africa could take the turn they had taken. The literary mood in more recent writings – Ayi Kwei Armah's *The Beautyful Ones Are Not Yet Born*, Chinua Achebe's *A Man of the People*, Okot p'Bitek's *Song of Lawino*, Okello Oculi's *Prostitute* and *The Orphan*, is one of disillusionment: we have scorched the snake of colonialism, not killed it. Or rather colonialism was one of the myriad skins the snake can put on.

The real snake was surely monopoly capitalism, whose very condition of growth is cut-throat competition, inequality, and oppression of one group by another. It was capitalism and its external manifestations, imperialism, colonialism, neo-colonialism, that had disfigured the African past. For in order that one group, one race, one class (and mostly a minority) can exploit another group, race or class (mostly the majority), it must not only steal its body, batter and barter it for thirty pieces of silver, but must steal its mind and soul as well. Hence the oppressor's obsession with disfiguring a people's past and history. Through the school system, he can soothe the fears of the colonized, or make them at least connive at the rationale behind capitalist exploitation. 'Better than the cannon, it [the school] makes conquest permanent. The cannon compels the body, the school bewitches the soul.' So says Chiekh Hamidou Kane, in *Ambiguous Adventure*.

To gain the belief in ourselves that Achebe talks about, some of the younger African writers now realize not only that they must reclaim their past, but that the very condition of a successful and objective reclamation is the dismantling of all colonial institutions, and especially capitalism, as patterns of social and economic development. Capitalism, even at its most efficient, has failed to create equality and balanced human relationships in Europe and America. Why do we think it can work in Africa? African youth is rejecting the notion of a common African (racial) humanity, which remains the same irrespective of any social changes or any gross economic inequalities.

The African past is not only one of egalitarian peasant communities, and of empires rising and falling, but also one of continued exploitation at the hands of the West. That this exploitation is facilitated by the ruling classes, whether in the traditional African community or by the middle classes in the colonial era, does not make it any less devastating for the African psyche. This is the background, the reality, against which Africans are writing. Youth wants to create a new society reflected in Africa's educational, political, and economic structure. In their study of breakaway churches in East Africa, called *A Place to Feel at Home*, Professor Bethwell Ogot and Fred Welbourn have written:

If a home is destroyed, whether the material house or the relationship between those who inhabit it, a new home must be found or its individual members become insecure, maladjusted, alien society. If they are unlucky they go to the wall; if lucky they build for themselves afresh.[9]

I do not share Ogot's and Welbourn's faith in luck. I believe that the African masses will build a place to feel at home. For they are not alone. In Asia, in Latin America, in Black America, the people are fighting the same battle. I believe the African novelist, the African writer, can help in this struggle. But he must be committed on the side of the majority (as indeed he was during the anti-colonial struggle) whose silent and violent clamour for change is rocking the continent. By diving into himself, deep into the collective unconscious of his people, he can seek the root, the trend, in the revolutionary struggle. He has already done something in restoring the African character to his history, to his past. But in a capitalist society, the past has a romantic glamour: gazing at it, as witness Wordsworth, and D. H. Lawrence, or more recently Yukio Mishima of Japan, is often a means of escaping the present. It is only in a socialist context that a look at yesterday can be meaningful in illuminating today and tomorrow. Whatever his ideological persuasion, this is the African writer's task.

REFERENCES

1 Based on a paper given to the Kenya Historical Association (Nairobi Branch) 1968, and subsequently read at the Ife conference on African Writing, the same year.
2 George Lamming: *The Pleasures of Exile* (Joseph, London, 1960), p. 34.
3 Orlando Patterson: *An Absence of Ruins* (Hutchinson, London, 1967), p. 96.
4 V. S. Naipaul: *The Mimic Men* (Deutsch, London, 1967), p. 10.
5 V. S. Naipaul: *The Mimic Men*, p. 175.
6 Gideon Were: *The Survivors* (Equatorial Publishers, Nairobi, 1968), p. XIII.
7 Quoted by George Lamming: *The Pleasures of Exile*.
8 Okot p'Bitek: *Song of Lawino* (EAPH, Nairobi, 1967), p. 29.
9 B. A. Ogot and F. Welbourn *A Place to Feel at Home* (OUP, London, 1966), p. 133.

The Writer in a Changing Society[1]

▼▼▼▼▼▼▼▼▼▼▼▼▼▼▼▼▼▼▼▼▼▼▼▼▼▼

A writer responds, with his total personality, to a social environment which changes all the time. Being a kind of sensitive needle, he registers, with varying degrees of accuracy and success, the conflicts and tensions in his changing society. Thus the same writer will produce different types of work, sometimes contradictory in mood, sentiment, degree of optimism and even world-view. For the writer himself lives in, and is shaped by, history.

We can see this in the work of the Malawian poet and novelist, David Rubadiri. In 1952 he wrote his famous poem *Stanley Meets Mutesa*, in which he painted a picture of the fatal encounter between Africa and Europe and captured the mood of a continent. For this was a dominant theme in African writing. The period was also one of Africa's cultural and political assertion. Fourteen years later he was to write a novel, *No Bride Price*, which showed his distaste with the post-Independence era in Africa: the leaders of the anti-colonial struggle have become traitors to their peoples' cause and have sacrificed Africa on the altar of their own middle-class comfort. The disillusionment with the ruling élite is to be found in the recent works of most African writers: Okot p'Bitek, Leonard Kibera, Chinua Achebe, Wole Soyinka, Ayi Kwei Armah, to mention only a few. All of them are reacting to a situation very different from the one prevailing in the fifties.

I too must have changed since I started writing in 1960.

I was then a student at Makerere University College. I remember sending a shy little note to the Warden of my then Hall of Residence saying I wanted to be a writer. No doubt the note was a little hasty and rather self-conscious, because I had not then written anything. I had read a number of writers, African and West Indian, and I knew that what they told, the song they sang, was different from what I had heard from the British writers who had been crammed down my throat in schools and at the

University. The African writers spoke to me, they spoke about my situation. What was my situation?

I grew up in a small village. My father with his four wives had no land.
They lived as tenants-at-will on somebody else's land. Harvests were often
poor. Sweetened tea with milk at any time of day was a luxury. We had
one meal a day – late in the evening. Every day the women would go to
their scruffy little strips of shamba. But they had faith and they waited.

Just opposite the ridge on which our village was scattered were the
sprawling green fields owned by the white settlers. They grew coffee and
tea and pyrethrum. I worked there sometimes, digging the ground, tending
the settlers' crops, and this for less than ten shillings. Every morning African workers would stream across the valley to sell their sweat for such a
meagre sum of money, and at the end of the week or month they would
give it all to the Indian trader who owned most of the shops in our area
for a pound of sugar, maize flour, or grains, thankful that this would
silence the children's clamour for a few days. These workers were the
creators of wealth but they never benefited from it: the products of their
collective sweat went to feed and clothe the children of the Indian trader,
and those of the European settlers not only in our country but even those
in England. I was living in a village and also in a colonial situation.

One day I heard a song. I remember the scene so vividly: the women who
sang it are now before me – their sad faces and their plaintive melody. I
was then ten or eleven. They were being forcibly ejected from the land
they occupied and sent to another part of the country so barren that people
called it the land of black rocks. This was the gist of their song:

> And there will be great great joy
> When our land comes back to us
> For Kenya is the country of black people.
>
> And you our children
> Tighten belts around your waist
> So you will one day drive away from this land
> The race of white people
> For truly, Kenya is a black man's country.

They were in a convoy of lorries, caged, but they had one voice. They sang
of a common loss and hope and I felt their voice rock the earth where I
stood literally unable to move.

Their words were not the platitudes of our university philosophers who
use words as shields from life and truth: these women had lived the words

they spoke. There was at once a fatalistic acceptance of the inevitable and also a collective defiance. 'We shall overcome', they seemed to say. The women had taken a correct political stand in the face of an oppressive enemy.

In 1923 such a stand had cost the lives of twenty-three people in Nairobi when men and women collected and demanded the release of their leaders. That stand also cost the lives of our early heroes of resistance, like the Laibon of the Kalenjin people, who led a violent peasant resistance against the early British occupation. In 1952 that dogged collective resistance cost Kenya even more lives; the peasants had taken to the forest to defend their lives and property and for four years were able to withstand the military might of British imperialism.

That song I heard as a child then spoke of things past and things to come. I was living in a colonial situation but I did not know it. Not even when I went to school. I went to a missionary school where we were told over and over again that we were potential leaders of our people. We were being trained to be good responsible leaders. Education was not aimed at a knowledge of self and the reality of the black man's place in the world. What we did not know was that we were being groomed to become a buffer state between the propertied white rulers and the harsh realities under which the African peasants and workers lived. The idea was something like this. They, the African workers and peasants, would see their selected few brothers and sisters living in relative comfort and fraternizing with whites and they would be contented: they would have a we-have-almost-arrived kind of attitude – 'we are getting equality bit by bit.' Our schools and universities – I am not sure if they have changed much – were monuments of lies and half-truths. That which was most admired was a search for truth, meaning a life devoted to the truth that only rationalized the *status quo*, that conferred on nationally stolen property – stolen that is from the masses – the aura of sanctity. While we were at our bourgeois schools and universities searching for that truth in books written for us by our imperial conquerors, the peasant masses, those women I once heard sing, had collectively rejected the white seizure of the land.

It was they who fought for Uhuru. It was the united strength of the peasants and workers that made British imperialists retreat, even though they later returned through the back door.

What have these peasants gained from Uhuru? Has our ruling élite tried to change the colonial social and economic structure? Are the peasants and workers in control of the land they fought for?

When I look around me, I see sad faces, I see unfulfilled hope and promise. We who went to schools and colleges and had regular salaries were quickly able to buy positions among the middle classes. With our cars, lands, and mansions, we forget that we are only joining our European and Asian counterparts in living on the sweat of millions. We entered the race to fill some of the vacant places, silencing protest by assuring our followers that we were only getting the national cake – for the tribe. Even the pretence of a national ideal has been abandoned by the ruling élite. When hungry, unsatisfied voices clamour around us we only say: 'Hush! you might ruin our tribal chances of a bigger share in the national cake.'

The Biafran-Nigerian conflict, where ordinary men and women who had not in any case gained much from Uhuru were made to slaughter one another, with guns supplied by competing Western powers who had for centuries ravished the continent, is today's African reality: the potential of a Biafran type of conflict exists in every African country that has doggedly refused to dismantle capitalism and colonial economic structures, to correct the legacy of an uneven geographic and social development.

I believe that African intellectuals must align themselves with the struggle of the African masses for a meaningful national ideal. For we must strive for a form of social organization that will free the manacled spirit and energy of our people so we can build a new country, and sing a new song. Perhaps, in a small way, the African writer can help in articulating the feelings behind this struggle.

REFERENCES

1 Speech delivered to Makerere Extra-mural students at Jinja, Uganda, October, 1969.

Chinua Achebe:
A Man of the People[1]

▼▼▼▼▼▼▼▼▼▼▼▼▼▼▼▼▼▼▼▼▼▼▼▼▼▼▼▼▼▼▼

In 1964 Mr Chinua Achebe told a conference on Commonwealth Literature at Leeds that part of his business as a novelist was to teach, to re-educate his society out of their acceptance of racial inferiority.

'Here, then,' he said, 'is an adequate revolution for me to espouse – to help my society regain its belief in itself and put away the complexes of the years of denigration and self-denigration.'

The European presence in Africa is, of course, the origin of those complexes. Inflated with holy zeal, the missionaries rooted out their proselytes from African societies. Christian bigotry and misguided altruism was here at work. African society was labelled savage, and the destiny of those who dwelt therein was hell. The administrator, clearing the way – with fire and sword – for the settler and other commercial interests, held a similar attitude to the conquered races. In *Things Fall Apart* the District Commissioner, who, in the words of one of the characters, has driven Okonkwo, the greatest man in Umuofia, to kill himself, is a typical Crusoe blind to the possibility that Friday could be a complex being with a complex culture. Notice the title he has chosen, after much thought, for the book he is planning to write: *The Pacification of the Primitive Tribes of Lower Niger. Things Fall Apart* is Achebe's answer to years of Christian bigotry and Crusoe's naïve view of Friday.

The counterpart of the District Commissioner in modern Nigeria is Mr Greene, another administrator, who, in *No Longer At Ease*, believes that the African is corrupt through and through. This novel, in which Achebe explores the pressures, within and without, that cause a sensitive individual to fall from great heights and in the end succumb to the corruption he condemns, is another answer to the colonizer's over-simplifications. In the two novels, Achebe is reacting to the European presence and naïve view of Africa.

Such an approach to society had its limitations: or, the limitation lay in the novelist's attitude to his society rather than in the actual content and presentation. The teacher's prime concern was to correct the bias by re-creating the society – its strengths, weaknesses, triumphs, failures – for his pupils and a deluded world to see and learn. Here was a particular African society as it really was, he seemed to point out. The pupils rejoiced in their society's triumphs and mourned with its failures: they anxiously watched Obi Okonkwo gradually succumb to corruption despite his admirable principles and held back their tears with difficulty. They sighed and nodded their heads – in sympathy of course: they understood, where the District Commissioner and Mr Greene had failed to understand.

Note that Achebe was not concerned with merely dishing out blame: 'It is too late in the day,' he told the Conference, 'to get worked up about it or to blame others, much as they deserve such blame and condemnation. What we need to do is to look back and try to find out where we went wrong, where the rain began to beat us.'

Achebe's new novel, *A Man of the People*, attempts to do that: to find where the rain began to beat us. Hence it is doubly significant, for apart from confirming the author's mastery of technique and his succinct use of language (this time it has a relaxed warm flow), it marks a break with his earlier attitude. He has turned his back on the European presence. He no longer feels the need to explain, or point out mistakes, by merely recreating. The process, I believe, started with *Arrow of God*. But even there (though the teacher is not reacting to the colonizer's view of Africa he is in fact more interested in problems of power and responsibility) the teacher took his time, was patient with his pupils. What has happened in *A Man of the People* – the change in attitude to his audience – is something which can only be felt by following, through the earlier novels, Achebe's creative response to a rapidly changing society.

Now, in the new novel, the teacher talks to his pupils, directly. He has lost patience. He retains self-control in that he does not let anger drive him into incoherent rage and wild lashing. Instead he takes his satirical whip and raps his pupils – with anger, of course, sometimes with pathos verging on tears, but often with bitterness, though this is hardly discernible because below it flow compassion and a zest for life. His pupils are – or ought to be – disturbed. For in *A Man of the People* the teacher accuses them all of complicity in the corruption that has beset our society. *Your* indifference and cynicism has given birth to and nurtured Chief Nanga, he says.

Chief the Honourable M. A. Nanga, M.P., is a corrupt, uncultured Minister of Culture in a corrupt régime in an independent African State. In a country where the majority of the peasants and workers live in shacks and can afford only pails for excrement, the Minister lives in 'a princely seven bathroom mansion with its seven gleaming, silent action, water-closets'. He only arranges for particular roads to be tarred, with an eye to votes in the next election, to ensure the arrival of his buses – ten luxury buses supplied to him by the British Amalgamated on the 'never-never'. Elections are a mockery of democracy, with thuggery, violence and rigging allied to British commercial interests.

The relationship between the masses and the neo-colonial élite, so aptly described by Frantz Fanon in *The Wretched of the Earth*, as a pitfall of national consciousness is here brilliantly captured in the image of the rain and the house.

> We had all been in the rain together until yesterday. Then a handful of us – the smart and the lucky and hardly ever the best – had scrambled for the one shelter our former rulers left, and had taken it over and barricaded themselves in. And from within they sought to persuade the rest through numerous loudspeakers, that the first phase of the struggle had been won and that the next phase – the extension of our house – was even more important and called for new and original tactics; it required that all argument should cease and the whole people speak with one voice and that any more dissent and argument outside the door of the shelter would subvert and bring down the whole house.[2]

Everybody is caught up in this complicity with evil: the masses with their cynicism – 'Tell them that this man had used his position to enrich himself and they would ask you if you thought a sensible man would spit out the juicy morsel that good fortune had placed in his mouth' – and hardened indifference; and the élite – even people like Odili are shown as being perilously close to Nanga – with their greed, lack of creativity and pitiable dependence on their former colonial rulers. It is left to the army, in the novel, to halt what has become an intolerable position.

But is this a solution? Achebe-cum-teacher has left too many questions unanswered. Or maybe he has levelled his accusation, has raised questions, and left it to the pupils to find the answers. Can people like Obi Okonkwo, Nanga, Odili, Max – or political parties even like the Common People's Convention – behave in a radically different way while operating within and in fact espousing the same economic and social set-up? Here we are brought back to the image of the house. For what people like Odili, Max and the army have to offer is not the possibility of building a new house on a different kind of foundation, but of extending the old one. The novel seems to suggest the possibiltity of individual honesty, integrity and maybe greater efficiency in building the extension. However, a given organization of material interests dictates its own morality. Which do you change first in a society – its politico-economic base (new foundations for a new house of a different nature) or the morality of individual men and women?

The pupils, and the teachers as well, must define their attitude – and find solutions – to these questions. What Achebe has done in *A Man of the People* is to make it impossible or inexcusable for other African writers to do other than address themselves directly to their audiences in Africa – not in a comforting spirit – and tell them that such problems are their concern. The teacher no longer stands apart to contemplate. He has moved with a whip among the pupils, flagellating himself as well as them. He is now the true man of the people.

REFERENCES

1 A review of *A Man of the People* which appeared in *Omen* (October, 1966), a student magazine in Leeds University, edited by Grant Kamenju.
2 Chinua Achebe, *A Man of the People* (Heinemann, London, 1966), p. 42.

Wole Soyinka, T.M. Aluko and the Satiric Voice[1]

Satire takes for its province a whole society, and for its purpose, criticism. The satirist sets himself certain standards and criticizes society when and where it departs from these norms. He invites us to assume his standards and share the moral indignation which moves him to pour derision and ridicule on society's failings. He corrects through painful, sometimes malicious, laughter.

When discussing any satirist, then, we must see him in his social and political setting. In the case of Aluko and Soyinka this means looking at contemporary Africa and in particular at Nigeria. Independence, of course, is the most obvious feature of the present African scene. (Though in Angola, Mozambique, Zimbabwe and South Africa white racists and fascists still enslave the black population.) The phase of independence and post-independence adjustment is preceded by others, but we shall concern ourselves with two.

The first is the stage of colonial conquest. Economic and political institutions are moulded on those of the metropolitan power. The aim is to create the good docile native – a willing source of raw material and cheap labour. And if he is not willing? One can always rely on the police and the army to do a little pacification. So that through fear of the Bible or the sword, the native at first acts as if he accepts the situation. The educational institutions – remember the Church – attempt to strengthen his faith in the *status quo*. The native is a clean slate on which anything can be scribbled. He is subjected to a constant barrage of suggestions that Western culture is all. France went further than Britain: she wanted so to scribble on the slate that all the black surface would be covered with the white chalk of French culture. But some of these weapons of conquest, education for instance, are double-edged. The people watch the institutions of the master, noting their weaknesses: the disparity between religious ideals and practice, between the economic power of the white, often settler, minority and that of the black majority. The peasants and urban workers feel the pinch of taxation and appalling living conditions.

The second period is that of colonial rebellion. The masses are restive. The nationalist leaders, usually from the ranks of the educated few, organize the discontent into a weapon aimed at the throat of the master. 'Go unto Pharoah and say to him, Let my people go.' Often the nationalist élite demands independence in terms of the very Western ideals it was taught at school and in colonial universities. As Frantz Fanon has pointed out, the nationalist élite and the colonial administration quarrel in, and speak, a language they both understand – using phrases such as 'the rights of man', 'the sanctity of private property', etc. – while all about them, the workers and peasants clamour simply for bread and clothes. Eventually, either through violence, as in Kenya, or through 'peaceful' means, as in Nigeria, the national élite gains power, but only after it has promised to respect Prospero's values.

What does this independence mean? For the peasants and the urban workers this is a period of gradual disillusionment. Independence has not given them back their land. They are still without food and clothes. But now there is a difference. Before independence basic realities were boldly and visibly delineated: all conflicts were reduced to two polarities – white was wealth, power and privilege; black was poverty, labour and servitude. 'Remove the white man,' cried the nationalist leaders, 'and the root cause of our troubles is gone.' Gone? Not exactly! The peasants and workers are still the hewers and carriers, but this time, for what Aluko would call the 'black White Man'. Who will now be the scapegoat? The nationalist élite deflects from itself the never-silent clamours for better living conditions by fanning the flames of tribalism: the Yoruba is made to blame the enterprising Ibo; the Ibo is made to blame the uneducated Hausa; and the Hausa is made to blame the cunning Southerners. Class consciousness, transcending the vertical divisions of clan and tribe, would make the workers and peasants realize that they are all in a similar predicament, but up till now it has been stifled by nationalistic sentiments. Nationalism is not an ideology. Too often it falsely appeals to the camaraderie of the skin. Now, and this is a glimmer of hope, the masses are realizing that Blackness is not all.

For the élite, however, independence is a boon. Under the banner of Africanization, it grabs at jobs in the civil service and jostles for places on the directing boards of all the foreign companies – Shell, I.C.I., Unilever, Union Minière, Anglo-American banks and mining-corporations that really run the economy of the country. It surrounds itself with country houses, cars, washing machines, television sets and all the consumer durables that are associated with an acquisitive middle-class. In his latest novel, *A Man of the People*, Chinua Achebe has, in chief Nanga, delineated a typical representative of the emergent bourgeoisie.

How have Aluko and Soyinka reacted to it?

Aluko's first novel, *One Man, One Wife*, came out in 1959. It deals with the clash between Christianity – 'this one man, one wife religion' – and local polygamous culture. This collision of values, which took place all over Africa, has been the subject of many African novels, the best being Achebe's *Things Fall Apart*. Unlike Achebe, Aluko does not imaginatively capture the complexity of the encounter between the new and the old. He sees the conflict too much on one plane, the cultural, and does not emphasize its social and economic basis enough.

His second novel, *One Man, One Matchet*, which came out in 1964, is more successful. The characters are satirical illustrations of stereotyped attitudes, but they are fairly lively. The story is set in the second phase I talked about: when peasants, often led by urban workers, are restive and nationalist leaders are challenging colonial authority. It is the period when the British are trying to buy the co-operation of the emergent bourgeoisie. The retiring District Officer in the novel puts it this way: 'You'll remember the keynote of last year's second Wiltshire Course. In all we do we must carry the intelligentsia with us.' Cocoa, the main cash crop in Nigeria, is attacked by a disease whose cure is not known. A European Agricultural Officer newly arrived from England advises that to save the crop from destruction all the trees that show symptoms of the disease must be cut down. The village is immediately torn between those who want to comply with the government's decision and those who want to defend their 'tree of wealth'. One of the puzzled opponents speaks for all the others when he asks a series of sceptical, rhetorical questions:

The cocoa trees are ill, do you all hear that? Do you all hear that trees are ill? Does disease not make man himself go ill? Does death not kill man himself? And does disease not catch the White Man himself? And did a white man not die the other day – was his brother the white doctor able to save him? No one was able to save him because that day on which he died was his appointed day to go back to the Land of the Dead. Before he was conceived and born by his mother did he not promise the gods that he would return to them that day? Can anyone change that appointed day? . . . Can the White Man himself in all his knowledge change the appointed day? If therefore we cannot prevent a man from dying why should we worry so much because a tree is dying? If one dies, can we not plant a seed from which another will grow?[2]

His series of questions ends in a passionate rejection of the government proposals. Gradually politicians, European expatriates, village farmers and a new African District Officer are drawn into the conflict, in which the only cry is for 'One man, one matchet', 'One woman, one stick', 'One child, one stone', – an obvious travesty of the nationalist slogan: 'one man, one vote'.

Everything in this novel, although it is set in an earlier period, carries overtones of the violence, corruption and anarchy of contemporary Nigerian politics. But the treatment of the rivalry and challenge is satirical. The European characters are conceived as hollow in their smug faith in the efficacy of British parliamentary democracy. The young Agricultural Officer is impatient and wants Africans who oppose his policy to be jailed for standing in the way of progress.

> These bloody Africans need to be protected against themselves, and against their own ignorance. And, damn it, they need to be protected against our fancy notions of democracy. Just because we in Britain have evolved a system of government by discussion and argument which somehow seems to work we think we must use the same methods in tropical Africa. We think we must get agreement on every measure before we take decisions. But, what's the good of discussion by fellows who don't understand what we are talking about, and persist in misunderstanding our motive?[3]

The older District Officer, Mr Stanfield, is more patient: in the best liberal tradition – patronage and condescension:

> Parliamentary democracy, Henry, is the one great contribution that our country has made to civilization. It is for this that Britain will be remembered long after our empire has passed away.[4]

The new African District Officer, Udo Akpan, who speaks of tackling problems in an essentially African way and yet talks and acts like any white expatriate, is soon described as 'the black White Man' by his opponents. He is a graduate of Cambridge with an upper second in Classics, and of course, a Cambridge cricket blue. He is a perfect example of the African élite whose self-appointed task is to make colonialism work.

But the man who gets the biggest lashing is a rabble-rousing politician who exploits the ignorance of the illiterate masses to line his own pockets. Mr Benjamin Benjamin urges people to resist paying taxes, to resist cutting down trees, and persuades them to undertake a lawsuit for the recovery of land which they claim to be theirs, but which obviously belongs to a neighbouring tribe. His love of long words and fine flourishes, his use of public platforms and public issues to gain personal power, his hypocrisy in whatever he does, are the main object of Aluko's satire. Here is Aluko's description of him on the platform:

> The man rose to speak. First he put down his walking-stick. Then he took out of the breast pocket of his jacket a yellow handkerchief. Next he removed the glasses from his face and proceeded to wipe the lenses with the handkerchief. He replaced the glasses, removed the pipe from his mouth, and picked up the walking-stick again. Finally he began to speak, in English, but through [the court clerk].[5]

The duel between Benjamin Benjamin and Okpan, 'the black White Man,' is really the story of Aluko's novel. But Aluko's satire is ponderous. It lacks the bite which can expose a social miasma mainly because he does not really know what he wants. Amid his cry of 'One man, one matchet', and his delineation of the peasants as merely ignorant, incapable, and half-savage, we perhaps hear more the voice of cynicism which can't see the way ahead for Nigeria. Aluko's sympathies seem to lie, not with the peasants and workers, who after all are the main objects of colonial exploitation, but with Udo Akpan, who is incapable of seeing that the whole system he is trying to work is wrong, that it is no good just criticizing one or two anomalies in the machine. Colonialism is the child of capitalism. Until the whole structure is changed so that peasants and workers have an effective voice, decolonization will never be complete and we shall not even have started on the road to Independence.

Wole Soyinka is primarily a dramatist. He has published seven plays and one novel, and has contributed poems to journals all over the world. Like Achebe and Aluko, Soyinka is dissatisfied with the new men of power. He has no patience with what Frantz Fanon, in his book *The Wretched of the Earth*, has described as the shocking, anti-national ways of 'a bourgeoisie which is stupidly, contemptibly, cynically bourgeois'.[6] He is particularly incensed with the hypocrisy of religious leaders and with the ineffectuality and sheer apathy of the intellectuals. Brother Jero is the best representative of religious hypocrisy. He is heavily built, neatly bearded, and has thick but well-combed hair. He walks with a diviner's rod. The action of the play *The Trials of Brother Jero* takes place on a beach where various religious groups – the Brotherhood of Jero, the Cherubims and Seraphims, the Sisters of Judgement Day, and even the Heavenly Cowboys – compete for territory and converts. At some stage in the past the Town Council has had to intervene to mark out the spheres of influence. Brother Jero, like Volpone in Ben Jonson's comedy, is a cunning rogue who lives from cheating gullible fools out of their money. Because he has no illusions about his calling and, like England's Great Train Robbers, does his job with admirable skill, he is quite appealing. In the opening scene of the play, Brother Jero speaks about the situation on the beach with candid realism and characteristic self-mockery:

I'm a prophet. A prophet by birth and by inclination. You have probably seen many of us on the streets, many with their own churches, many inland, many on the coast, many leading processions, many looking for processions to lead, many curing the deaf, many raising the dead. In fact, there are eggs and there are eggs. Same thing with prophets. I was born a prophet. I think my parents found that I was born with rather thick and long hair. It was said to come right down to my eyes and down to my neck. For them, this was a certain sign that I was born a natural prophet. And I grew to love the trade. It used to be a very respectable one in those days and competition was dignified. But in the last few years, the beach has become fashionable, and the struggle for land has turned the thing into a thing of ridicule. Some prophets I could name gained their present beaches by getting women penitents to shake their bosoms in spiritual ecstasy. This prejudiced the councillors who came to divide the beach among us.

Yes, it did come to the point where it became necessary for the Town Council to come to the beach and settle the Prophets' territorial warfare once and for all. My Master, the same who brought me up in prophetic ways staked his claim and won a grant of land . . . I helped him, with a campaign led by six dancing girls from the French territory, all dressed as Jehovah's Witnesses. What my old Master did not realize was that I was really helping myself.[7]

Brother Jero and his fellow prophets represent the many political leaders that crop up in most African states, whose main object is to profit themselves at the expense of the masses. Brother Jero retains his followers by keeping them spiritually dissatisfied and thus in continual need of help.

I am glad I got here before any customers – I mean worshippers – well, customers if you like. I always get that feeling every morning that I am a shop-keeper waiting for customers. The regular ones come at definite times. Strange, dissatisfied people. I know they are dissatisfied because

I keep them dissatisfied. Once they are full, they won't come again. Like my good apprentice, Brother Chume. He wants to beat his wife, but I won't let him. If I do, he will become contented, and then that's another of my flock gone for ever.[8]

Some of Jero's followers are Members of Parliament, and one of them, from the Federal House of Assembly, wants him to prophesy that he'll become a Minister of War.

But it is the intellectual class in Nigeria, our academic gentlemen in their university ties and gowns, that Soyinka scorns most. He sees them as having neglected their rightful role of speaking out for the truth. Instead, they either approve of the *status quo*, rationalizing away all its corruption, or else they condone it by their silence. The moral atrophy of the intellectual is a theme occurring in most of Soyinka's plays, but it is particularly well illustrated in *A Dance of the Forests*, which he wrote and produced for the celebration of Nigerian independence. At one stage in the play the Forest Dwellers show the Human Community a scene from the Court of Mata Kharibu, a corrupt king in the time of the great Ghana and Mali empires. It is a warning to the present generation, as many of the characters in the court are recognizable among them also. At the King's court there is trouble, for the army captain refuses to go to war to recover the Queen's clothes from the husband she has just left. The physician tries to persuade the warrior to change his mind, but to no avail.

WARRIOR: It is an unjust war. I cannot lead my men into battle merely to recover the trousseau of any woman.

PHYSICIAN: Ah. But do you not see? It goes further than that. It is no longer the war of the queen's wardrobe. The war is now an affair of honour.

WARRIOR: An affair of honour? Since when was it an honourable thing to steal the wife of a brother chieftain?

PHYSICIAN: Can you really judge the action of another?

WARRIOR: No. But the results, and when they affect me and men who place their trust in me. If the king steals another's wife, it is his affair. But let it remain so. Mata Kharibu thought, hoped that the dishonoured king would go to war on her account. There he was wrong. It seems that her rightful husband does not consider that your new queen is worth a battle. But Mata Kharibu is so bent on bloodshed that he sends him a new message. Release the goods of this woman I took from you if there will be peace between us. Is this the action of a ruler who values the peace of his subjects?[9]

Most of you will recognize the familiar ring of this argument in the contemporary world situation. Today America – a great military power – is massacring the Vietnamese peasants on a scale revolting to the conscience of mankind. For Johnson, who is unable to put his own house in order – give reality to democracy in America and give black people their basic rights as American citizens – sees this unjust, unnecessary genocide as an affair of honour. The intellectuals at the court of Mata Kharibu, like those around Johnson in the White House, are called in to rationalize and justify the war.

HISTORIAN: Nations live by strength; nothing else has meaning. You only throw your life away uselessly.

MATA KHARIBU: (apprehensive.) Did you find anything?

HISTORIAN: There is no precedent, your Highness.

MATA KHARIBU: You have looked thoroughly?

HISTORIAN: It is unheard of. War is the only consistency that past ages afford us. It is the legacy which new nations seek to perpetuate. Patriots are grateful for wars. Soldiers have never questioned bloodshed. The cause is always the accident your majesty, and war is the Destiny. This man is a traitor. He must be in the enemy's pay.

MATA KHARIBU: He has taken sixty of my best soldiers with him.

HISTORIAN: Your Highness has been too lenient. Is the nation to ignore the challenge of greatness because of the petty-mindedness of a few cowards and traitors?

WARRIOR: I am no traitor!

HISTORIAN: Be quiet Soldier! I have here the whole history of Troy. If you were not the swillage of pigs and could read the writings of wiser men, I would show you the magnificence of the destruction of a beautiful city. I would reveal to you the attainments of men which lifted mankind to the ranks of gods and demi-gods. And who was the inspiration of this divine carnage? Helen of Troy, a woman whose honour became as rare a conception as her beauty. Would Troy, if it were standing today lay claim to preservation in the annals of history if a thousand valiant Greeks had not been slaughtered before its gates, and a hundred thousand Trojans within her walls? Do you, a mere cog in the wheel of Destiny, cover your face and whine like a thing that is unfit to lick a soldier's boots, you, a Captain . . . Your Majesty, I am only the Court historian and I crave your august indulgence for any excess of zeal. But history has always revealed that the soldier who will not fight has the blood of slaves in him. For the sake of your humble subjects, this renegade must be treated as a slave.[10]

So the captain and his army are going to be sold into slavery, but not before the Court historian has made a private arrangement with the slave-trader to get his share of the profit. Later on the historian invites the physician for a drink.

> You are a learned man and I would appreciate an opportunity to discuss the historial implications of this . . . mutiny . . . if one can really call it that . . . We were so near to the greatness of Troy and Greece . . . I mean this is war as it should be fought . . . over nothing . . . do you not agree?[11]

Not surprisingly, Soyinka portrays the ineffectuality of the intellectual in sexual terms. He is effeminate, lacks virility: his head is stuffed with bits and pieces of Western culture. There is Lakunle, the school teacher in *The Lion and the Jewel*, a cowardly braggart, who loses his betrothed to Baroka, a traditional chief. Lakunle's culturedness consists of his opposition to bride-price and his dreams of dance-halls where even old women can learn the waltz and the foxtrot, and I suppose, learn to kiss like Christians and other educated people! There is also Faseyi in *The Interpreters*, a highly qualified doctor, a lecturer at the university. He lives in constant terror of losing his respectability and fawns on all those who have even the slightest claim to power or influence. In the passage which follows, Faseyi and his wife – a sweet-natured English girl – have been invited to a party at the house of an Ambassador where they are to be presented:

> Monica Faseyi was always in disgrace. And so at the entrance to the embassy reception her husband stopped and inspected her thoroughly. Satisfied, he nodded and quickly checked the line of his own bow-tie. He smiled then and kissed her formally on the forehead.
>
> 'You might as well put on your gloves now.'
>
> 'What gloves? I didn't bring any.'
>
> Faseyi thought she was teasing, and out of character though it was, Monica was certain that her husband was teasing.
>
> 'Come on now, put on the gloves.'
>
> 'You stop teasing now. Who do you see wearing gloves in Nigeria?'
>
> Faseyi was no longer joking. He had snatched the handbag from her and found that there were no gloves inside. 'Do you mean you didn't bring them?'
>
> 'Bring what, Ayo?'
>
> 'The gloves of course. What else?'
>
> 'But I haven't any gloves. I gave the ones I had away soon after I came.'

'I am not talking about two years ago. I mean the gloves you've bought for tonight.'

'I didn't buy any. Ayo, what's all this?'

'What's all this? I should ask you what's all this! Didn't I give you an invitation over a week ago?'

'Yes you did, but . . .'

'Darling, I gave you a cheque for fifteen pounds to get yourself all you needed.'

'I thought you wanted me to have a new dress.'

'For heaven's sake, what about the gloves?'

'But you didn't say anything about gloves.'

'Was it necessary to say anything? It was right there on the card. In black and white.' He took the card from his pocket, dragged it from the envelope and thrust it under her eyes. 'Read it, there it is. Read it.'

Monica read the last line on the card. 'But Ayo, it only says those who are to be presented. We are not, are we?'

Ayo held his head. 'We *are* to be presented.'

'You didn't tell me. How was I to know?'

'How were you to know! It took me two weeks to wangle the presentation, and now you ask me how were you to know. What would be the whole point of coming if we were not to be presented?'

'I am sorry,' said Monica, 'it never occurred to me . . .'

'Nothing ever occurs to you! . . . But at least you could have used some initiative. Even if there was no question of being presented, you knew Their Excellencies would be here.'

'I am sorry.'

'Darling, if the Queen was attending a garden party, would you go dressed without your gloves?'

'I've said I am sorry, Ayo. I really am. Perhaps I had better return home.'

'But would you? Answer my question. Would you attend the same party with the Queen without gloves.'

'I really don't know, Ayo. I never moved in such circles.'

'Darling, I am surprised at you. These are simple requirements of society which any intelligent person would know.' He looked at his watch, thinking rapidly, biting his lips in vexation. And then he hit a solution. 'Of course. Mummy will help out. She is bound to have a pair at home.'

The young girl with the mild voice said, 'No, Ayo. It's much simpler for me just to go back home.'

'What is the use if I cannot be presented with my wife? Let's go back for the gloves.'

'The reception will be over by the time we get back.'

The thought halted Faseyi definitely. 'All right, come on. But you will have to stay behind when we are called.'[12]

Does Faseyi have to bother with this kind of social rubbish, one of his friends asks? He is, after all, a qualified doctor. He can get a job anywhere. Actually Faseyi is portrayed as a figure arousing pity rather than anger. He stinks less, or differently from, the judges, the politicians, the business-men who, despite their relative wealth in a poor country, are prepared to wait for hours, burning in the sun, to get a small bribe – a drink maybe – from people who are not even employed.

The artist in Soyinka's world gets away unscathed. He is seen as the conscience of the nation. In *A Dance of the Forests* the Court poet is one of the few people who dares raise his voice whenever the king and his whorish queen overreach themselves. And Eman, the Christ-like figure in *The Strong Breed*, has an artist's sensitivity. He remains a stranger to the people: those who have much to give, he says, fulfil themselves in total loneliness. Certainly this is the lot of Sekoni, the civil engineer in *The Interpreters*. After completing a power station to which he has devoted much of his energy, thought, and vision, he is told by the Council that the station is not good enough, that it is not going to be used. It is not even going to be tested. We later discover that the Councillors had made an agreement with the contractors to break the contract, as this meant more money for them all. They were going to share out the loot from public funds. The shock breaks Sekoni. He turns to carving.

Confronted with the impotence of the élite, the corruption of those steering the ship of State and those looking after its organs of justice, Wole Soyinka does not know where to turn. Often the characters held up for our admiration are (apart from the artists) cynics, or sheer tribal reactionaries like Baroka. The cynicism is hidden in the language (the author seems to revel in his own linguistic mastery) and in occasional flights into metaphysics. Soyinka's good man is the uncorrupted individual: his liberal humanism leads him to admire an individual's lone act of courage, and thus often he ignores the creative struggle of the masses. The ordinary people, workers and peasants, in his plays remain passive watchers on the shore or pitiful comedians on the road.

Although Soyinka exposes his society in breadth, the picture he draws is static, for he fails to see the present in the historical perspective of conflict and struggle. It is not enough for the African artist, standing aloof, to view society and highlight its weaknesses. He must try to go beyond this, to seek out the sources, the causes and the trends of a revolutionary struggle which has already destroyed the traditional power-map drawn up by the colonialist nations. And Africa is not alone. All over the world the exploited majority, from the Americas, across Africa and the Middle East, to the outer edges of Asia, is claiming its own. The artist in his writings is not outside the battle. By diving into its sources, he can give moral direction and vision to a struggle which, though suffering temporary reaction, is continuous and is changing the face of the twentieth century.

REFERENCES

1 Talk originally given at Africa Centre, London, 1966 under the title 'Satire in Nigeria'.

2 T. M. Aluko: *One Man, One Matchet* (Heinemann, London, 1964), p. 5.

3 *One Man, One Matchet*, pp. 9–10.

4 *One Man, One Matchet*, p. 10.

5 *One Man, One Matchet*, p. 7.

6 Frantz Fanon: *The Wretched of the Earth*, (Penguin, London, 1967), p. 121.

7 Wole Soyinka: *The Trials of Brother Jero* (*Three Short Plays*, Oxford University Press, 1967) pp. 201–2.

8 *The Trials of Brother Jero*, p. 211.

9 Wole Soyinka: *A Dance of the Forests* (Oxford University Press, 1967), p. 54.

10 *A Dance of the Forests*, pp. 57–58.

11 *A Dance of the Forests*, p. 62.

12 Wole Soyinka: *The Interpreters* (Deutsch, London, 1965. Also Heinemann African Writers Series, London, 1970.) pp. 39–41.

Okot p'Bitek and writing in East Africa[1]

▼▼▼▼▼▼▼▼▼▼▼▼▼▼▼▼▼▼▼▼▼▼▼▼▼▼▼▼▼▼▼▼

In 1964 Taban Lo Liyong wrote to *Transition* and later to the *East African Journal* bitterly lamenting East Africa's literary barrenness: in classes and in discussion groups at his school in Iowa, USA, the names of Wole Soyinka, Chinua Achebe, J. P. Clark, Amos Tutuola, Christopher Okigbo, Lewis Nkosi, Alex la Guma, Ezekiel Mphahlele and others, were on everybody's lips. But not a name from East Africa.

Earlier, in 1962, East African writers – Jonathan Kariara, Rebecca Njau, John Nagenda, Okot p'Bitek, Grace Ogot, and myself – who attended the conference of African Writers at Makerere University, Kampala, Uganda, had certainly been overwhelmed by the literary turbulence in West Africa and Southern Africa. Although the conference was held on our courtyard, few of us had published anything between hard covers: were we not wearing false robes?

Not surprisingly, a certain avuncular air attended both the choice of venue and the conduct of the conference: it was time East Africa awoke and caught up with the rest. Chemchemi Cultural Centre, in the image of Mbari in Nigeria, was later started in Nairobi to help in the expected awakening. Ezekiel Mphahlele went round Kenya talking to schools, teacher training colleges, and at various community centres in Nairobi. Chemchemi, unlike the Mbari centres, did not take root. It quickly folded up, to be replaced by the Kariara-Njau inspired Paa Ya Paa.

Even today, and despite the novels, poetry, and plays published and at least two major publishing houses, there are people who still think of East Africa as a literary desert: anything of significant cultural and literary value has yet to emerge from that region, in their view.

Behind the avuncular attitudes, the native embarrassment, and Lo Liyong's laments, was an assumption that a people's literature could only be written in English or in other borrowed tongues. Swahili literature, after all, had a strong tradition going back three or four centuries. Students are only now discovering how rich this literature is, especially in epic poetry and praise songs. To musical accompaniment, the poets sang of Islamic wars, of their legendary heroes, while here and there they tucked in moral sermons. In modern times, Shabaan Roberts had published a huge quantity of poetry: by 1962 he was already a major Swahili poet. In 1954 Okot p'Bitek had published a modern novel *Lak Tar*, in Lwo. These aspects of the East African literary scene were hardly mentioned at the Kampala Conference.

We might also have asked ourselves what 'literature' was. Was it only that which has been written down in black and white? Put that way, it becomes apparent how inadequate the word is to define the verbal embodiment of a people's creative spirit. East Africa, like the rest of the continent, is rich in songs, poems and stories that go back to times immemorial, to Agu and Agu. During a recent debate on the need to abolish the colonial concept of an English Department, some lecturers in Nairobi put a very strong case for the inclusion and study of this rich and many-sided tradition. They said:

> (This) art did not end yesterday. Even now there are songs being sung in political rallies, in churches, in night clubs by guitarists, by accordion players, by dancers, etc. Another point to be observed is the interlinked nature of art forms in traditional practice. Verbal forms are not always distinct from dance, music etc. For example, in music there is close correspondence between verbal and melodic tones: in 'metrical lyrics', it has been observed that poetic text is inseparable from tune: and the 'folk tale' often bears an 'operatic' form, with sung refrain as an integral part. The distinction between prose and poetry is absent or very fluid. Though tale, dance, song, myth etc. can be performed for individual aesthetic enjoyment, they have other social purposes as well. The oral tradition . . . comments on society because of its intimate relationship and involvement.[2]

During the anti-colonial struggle new song-poems were created to express defiance and people's collective aspirations. Two examples will do. During the 'thirties, the Agikuyu of Kenya and the colonial missionaries came into conflict over the matter of female circumcision. The religious conflict was, of course, a reflection of the deeper political and economic struggle. People created a song-dance called Muthirigo, to discourage and ridicule those who sided with the missionaries. The following is a poor rendering of three verses:

I would never pay bride-wealth for an uncircumcised girl.
My mother is circumcised.
My father is circumcised.
A lamb whose tail is not cut
Cannot be used for sacrifice.

An uncircumcised girl is foolish.
And for you to know she is foolish
An infant's throat is blocked by a banana
And she falls down with laughter.

And if Wagakinya should die
Oh if Wagakinya should die
While you people take flowers to his funeral
I will take him a wreath of stinging nettles.

This was so popular and so effective that the colonial government banned it. Or consider the fifties: the outbreak of the Mau Mau liberation struggle was preceded by waves of song-poems. The jailhouse, one of the most important of the many repressive features of colonialism, was often seen as swallowing 'all our firstborn'. But in one of the songs the parents are asked to rejoice because God, right and justice would surely bring back the warriors. They ridiculed traitors (Thata Cia Bururi) and told them:

The barren of the earth are worthless animals
They betrayed us: we were taken
We were pushed into jailhouses, but
God is great, we shall overcome.

The braves of the black race were seen as coming back in a cloud of victory:

And when the heroes of the race return
Where will you run to, you barren ones!
You betrayed us, so we might suffer! But
God is great, we shall surely come back.

Again these song-poems were banned by the colonial regime. For here poetry and songs functioned as newspapers, as media for information and mutual encouragement. More recently, there has been an upsurge of new songs, popular sayings in rural areas and in urban slums, all commenting on various aspects of independence. Again so confining, so arrogantly exclusive is the word 'literature' that these types of creative expression are not discussed as representative of a people's cultural mainstream. It is because of this that Mr Pio Zirimu, a Ugandan linguist and literary critic, has coined the word 'orature'.

Now compared with that vital oral tradition, East African literature in borrowed Aryan tongues is very recent, although it is rapidly growing. Jomo Kenyatta's book *Facing Mount Kenya* stands in a rather equivocal position in this growth. It is not a work of literary imagination, certainly not a creative biography like Mphahlele's *Down Second Avenue* or Peter Abraham's *Tell Freedom*, yet it is not pure anthropology. It has energy, passion, and a real tension between the objective needs of his descriptive case-study of an African culture and his subjective commitment to the African struggle for freedom and self-identity: he even skilfully exploits myth to drive home his message. Most outstanding is the story of the man whose house was forcefully occupied by Mr Elephant after the man had in his kindness sheltered the jungle gentleman from the rain. A Commission of Inquiry consisting of other animals was appointed to look into the man's grievances, and decided, after careful deliberation, that the house really belonged to Mr Elephant. The message was clear: the Africans could never hope to obtain justice against Kenya settlers by appealing to the conscience of the oppressor or to that of his kith and kin. More important, the story and the book presage Mau Mau, the one historical trauma that has left an indelible mark on the quality of life and literature in Kenya.

In a violent revolutionary situation, the most honoured conventional loyalties are questioned: brother is pitted against brother, father against son. But also the most beautiful love, the most splendid courage and the most selfless total commitment to a just social cause are suddenly seen in entirely unexpected men, women and children. The majority of the people may often feel enveloped in a nightmare they can only dimly comprehend. Not surprisingly, few Kenyan writers have been able to ignore Mau Mau and the challenge of violence.

Muga Gacaru's autobiography, *Land of Sunshine*, tells of his experiences as a squatter on the European settlers' farms and ends with the outbreak of the armed liberation struggle in 1952. Mugo Gatheru, in *A Child of Two Worlds*, finds that even in his absence in India, Europe and America in search of education he could never get in colonial Kenya; Mau Mau and violence stalk him: the British agents want him repatriated to Kenya because of his supposed involvement in the political struggle. J. M. Kariuki's *Mau Mau Detainee* is really a praise song, in restrained prose edged with humour, to the courage and the dogged determination of those detained in various concentration camps. Other autobiographies tell of the Waruhiu Itote fight in the forest (Waruhiu Itote: *Mau Mau General*) and of the women's part in the struggle (Grace Waciuma: *Daughter of Mumbi*). Many of the novels, including my own, are in a similar vein. Godwin Wachira in *Ordeal in the Forest* recreates the life of four boys during the war. Leonard Kibera and Samuel Kahiga, in their tough collection of short stories, *Potent Ash*, tell of confused, often conflicting loyalties of smashed hopes and expectations, and of the enduring though strained relationships of the ordinary men and women during and even after the Mau Mau phase of the struggle. They write about the small man: they show the dignity of the poor and the wretched of the earth, despite the violence of body and feeling around them. Even when they write of the post-independence era, internal and external violence is around the corner. In this respect Kibera's story *The Spider's Web* is worth mentioning because it sets the tone for much of the recent prose output. Ngotho, working for his new masters (black like himself, since independence has now arrived), is slapped on the face by a girl who once, as an ordinary teacher in the village, had won fame and the nickname of 'Queen' for standing up to, and hitting back at an arrogant European Lady. As Ngotho works in the Queen's house, he cannot help reflecting on the past and on the meaning of Uhuru for workers, ordinary people, like himself. He remembers how 'everybody had sworn that they were going to build something together, something challenging and responsible, something that would make a black man respectable in his own country'. He, at first, 'had been willing to serve, to keep up the fire that had eventually smoked out the white man'. But now he feels that somehow a common goal has been lost sight of. 'He could not help but feel that the warriors had laid down their arrows and had parted different ways to fend for themselves.' This is why Ngotho is bitter. His objective social position has not changed in any way despite the exit of the visible white presence. The same class remains – this time in black skins. One of the most painful and shocking aspects of the story is the way the new occupants of the old European mansions so easily accept and demand privileges – symbolized by the Queen's acceptance of the title *Memsahib*. Yet they come from the same village: he is really her father. Even tradition (i.e. the father-daughter relationship) is violated when the hand that once defiantly hit 'the white lady' now hits Ngotho across the mouth. (You can imagine her about to shout: 'Africans are born lazy!') He ends up by stabbing his new master.

Violence, then, is an important feature of writing in East Africa, even when such works do not directly deal with Mau Mau. Robert Serumaga's novel *Return to the Shadows* reeks of the violence and blood of the 1966

Uganda Crisis: that is, the armed conflict between feudalistic forces led by the Kabaka and the progressive nationalism of Milton Obote. Hussein's play *Kinjekitile* is set during the Maji Maji armed resistance to German rule in Tanzania. The German imperialists slaughtered many Tanzanian peasants, as the British were to do later in Kenya. In the stories of Grace Ogot, *Land Without Thunder*, and in David Rubadiri's novel *No Bride Price*, the tensions, sometimes violent, of post-independence adjustment inform the tone and the narratives. Grace Ogot is especially aware of the internal emotional violence, as in the story of the secretary who resists her new boss's attempt to seduce her in the office – after work. *No Bride Price*, like Chinua Achebe's *A Man of the People*, ushered in the era of coups d'etat and military take-overs in African literature.

Yet another feature that marks out East African stories and novels is a tremendous awareness of the land. This is always evoked with loving tenderness, even in novels that are primarily urban in tone and in setting. In Kenya this is natural, since the land question has always been at the heart of the matter. But even in Uganda, the rural landscape is the background of literary sensibility. The most telling passage in Okello Oculi's novel *Prostitute* is when the betrayed heroine, outside her slum shack in Kampala, is recalling scenes from her rural village, going back to her peasant roots. People, whether the Padre, the Catechist, or Rebecca's mother with her well-known tongue are firmly rooted in the soil. The heroine especially recalls her girlhood with Rebecca – jumping and leaping and laughing in the hollows between the heavy heaps of fallen leaves and shreds of banana stems:

When sunset came and found us in the woods, among the trees and the bushes and the thorns and the pebbles and rock boulders, the red rays from the flaming face of the sun, sitting there in the West sliding away slowly but surely with that inevitable goodbye wave that makes parting such melancholy happening: a sudden tingle and tickle would come on that girl's body. She would want to run at those moments. She itched and jerked all over and could not contain the urge. She would start running towards the horizon with the sun. She ran and skipped, pulling her legs away and struggling with the grasses below her knees and high against her body. She ran and halted and clicked her tongue against the hold of the grasses against her speed. She ran and sang. Some women who were around sometimes would say that Rebecca was possessed by a spirit that wanted to take her to the sun. When she ran and I chased her and we both grew tired of running, she would fall down on the nearest sandy spot she saw and start grouping and collecting sands together into heaps.[3]

The memory of rural childhood, of the moon, of the sun, of the rivalry between darkness and moonlight, of the daytime wind that blows houses down and carries large pillars of dust into the sky – this the urban squalor and body degredation cannot take from her. These things are a part of her: they make life somehow bearable. In Rubadiri's *No Bride Price* a similarly evoked village life with roots in the soil is counterpoised against an urban setting that breaks loyalties, breeds incest and wrecks people's inner life. Grace Ogot's migrants to Tanzania in her novel *The Promised Land* are in search of new pastures and new lands. But they too are always conscious of the pumpkin in the homestead to which they inevitably return.

So far the East African novel has not radically departed from the Western mainstream. There has been little experimentation in language or in structure, or in the narrative method, except perhaps in the case of Okello Oculi, who freely moves from prose to poetry in the same novel.

This is true even in poetry. T. S. Eliot, W. B. Yeats, Gerard Manley Hopkins, William Wordsworth – these sources are the main inspiration for our poets, so they themselves say in the first anthology of East African poetry, *Drumbeat*. This influence, may I hasten to add, does not necessarily produce poetry of a lower quality than the home-grown variety. Jonathan Kariara and David Rubadiri, for instance, must rank among the finest poets in Africa. The lyrical voice of Kariara always evokes the beauty of the country and its people: the strength, the integrity and the endurance of the women especially. A lyrical tenderness characterises his lines when talking of the peasant mothers from whence we all came:

They bathe when the moon is high
Soft and fecund
Splash cold mountain stream water on their nipples
Drop their skin and call obscenities.[4]

In his poetry an outside force is seen as threatening the integrity of village life: it may be Christianity, or colonialism, or the brash new ways that come with the white clay of foreign education, stifling the black man inside. 'Doctor, what ails me, what ails?' David Rubadiri, with deceptive simplicity, can capture the mood of an important moment in history – like that fatal encounter between Stanley, the hired mercenary of international capitalism, and Mutesa, the tyrant king of feudal Buganda. A foreboding note of uncertainty is struck, without hysteria, in that moment's silence of assessment as the gates of reed are flung open and the West is let in. The whole poem is almost an exercise in understatement. Yet he suggests much tension in such lines as those describing the cool suspicious welcome the white man's entourage receives from women and children hidden behind banana groves and reed fences. These are:

No women to wail a song
Or drums to greet the white ambassador,
Only a few silent nods
From a few aged faces
Only a rumbling peal of drums
To summon Mutesa's court to parley.[5]

In other poems Rubadiri reminds us that the tide from the West that washes Africa to the bone once washed a wooden cross.

All these poets, including the younger ones – Samuel Mbure, Jared Angira, Richard Ntiru – sing with their own individual voices. Nevertheless, we can, I think, generalize and say that the poets, like their counterparts in fiction, have not in the past sufficiently explored the technical resources of the oral tradition or realised that these can revitalize their poetry and enable them to move in a different direction.

At least this was the position until 1967. And then came Okot p'Bitek with his long poem *Song of Lawino*. First written in Lwo and then translated into English by the author, *Song of Lawino* is a satiric assault on the African middle-class élite that has so unabashedly embraced Western bourgeois values and modes of life. Lawino, a peasant, is married to Ocol, who after acquiring Western education, abandons his rural world for urban artificiality, pretence and greed. His mistress, Clementine, the symbol of his new world, distorts her figure, straightens her hair, reddens her lips, bleaches her skin, pads her breasts – all in a feverish pursuit of a Western ideal of beauty and accomplishment. Lawino denounces her husband, ridicules the world he has chosen and proudly asserts the primacy of her peasant values and cultural symbols. In the process, she comments on every aspect of life in East Africa – dances, dresses, food, religion, education and politics. Lawino is not rejecting the validity of Western culture: to her every culture is valid to the community and the conditions that created it. What gnaws at her is the self-hatred that makes the Ocols totally reject and even consciously repudiate their roots in the African peasant world: they even go further and uncritically accept the half-digested mannerisms of a European bourgeois. Lawino cannot understand how Ocol could have been so quickly torn from his roots, because:

> . . . Only recently
> We would sit close together touching each other!
> Only recently I would play
> On my bow-harp
> Singing praises to my beloved.[6]

What she is describing is the whole alienating effect of Western education: people are educated not so that they may be re-integrated into the masses, help the community to raise their productive and cultural resources, join them in their struggle for total liberation, but to form a screen between the community and objective reality. One aspect of this reality is, of course, the continued exploitation of the Lawinos of the African world by the West and its class allies in Africa.

A few critics have reacted against what they see as her jealousy-motivated defence of every aspect of tradition. They thus turn the fundamental opposition between two value-systems into a mere personal quarrel between Lawino and her husband. We must in fact see the class basis of her attack: Lawino is the voice of the peasantry and her ridicule and scorn is aimed at the class basis of Ocol's behaviour. The poem is an incisive critique of bourgeois mannerisms and colonial education and values. For it is Ocol's education, with the values it inculcates in him, that drives him away from the community. With its critical realism the poem qualifies as a major contribution to African literature. Like Fanon on the subject of the pitfalls of national consciousness in *The Wretched of the Earth*, Lawino is asking Ocol to consciously negate and repudiate the social calling that the colonial legacy has bequeathed to the African intelligentsia. The significance of *Song of Lawino* in East Africa's literary consciousness lies not only in this ruthless exposure of the hollowness and lack of originality of a colonial middle class but also in its form. The author has borrowed from the song in the oral tradition. The African song gets its effect from an accumulation of details, statements and imagery, and in the variation of the tone and attitude of the poet-reciter to the object of praise. Lawino employs all these tactics in her dispraise of Ocol. *Song of Lawino* is the one poem that has mapped out new areas and new directions in East African poetry. It belongs to the soil. It is authentically East African in its tone and in its appeal. This can be seen in its reception: it is read everywhere, arousing heated debates. Some critics have even attempted a psychoanalysis of the creator of Lawino. It is the first time that a book of modern poetry has received such popular widespread acclaim. The effect on the young poets has been no less stunning, though a trifle dangerous. Many want to write like Okot p'Bitek. Unfortunately some have been taken in by its deceptive simplicity.

I said that *Song of Lawino* maps out a new literary direction in East
Africa. I should rather have said that it belongs to a new mood. It is part
of a movement. Other writers like Taban Lo Liyong in *Fixions* and Okello
Oculi in *The Orphan*, quite independently of Okot p'Bitek, have exploited
myths, rhythms and narrative techniques in African 'orature' with differing
degrees of success: but where they are successful the results are often
startling and brilliant.

Song of Lawino also belongs to a new mood of self-questioning and self-
examination, to find out where the rain began to beat us. Lawino, looking
around, finds that the warring political parties fundamentally represent
the bourgeios class interests and says:

I do not understand
The meaning of Uhuru
I do not understand
Why all the bitterness
And the cruelty
And the cowardice,
The fear,
The deadly fear
Eats the hearts
Of the political leaders!
Is it the money?
Is it the competition for position?

Someone said
Independence falls like a buffalo
And the hunters
Rush to it with drawn knives,
Sharp, shining knives
For carving the carcass.
And if your chest
Is small, bony and weak
They push you off
And if your knife is blunt
You get the dung on your elbow
But come home empty-handed
And the dogs bark at you.[7]

She finds herself unable to wholly identify with either of the two warring
parties, mainly because none represents her real interests. Why can't they
join hands to eradicate the real foe of Africa?

And while the pythons of sickness
Swallow the children
And the buffaloes of poverty
Knock the people down
And ignorance stands there
Like an elephant.

The war leaders
Are tightly locked in bloody feuds
Eating each other's liver . . .[8]

This is the mood captured in another poem, *Building the Nation,* by Henry
Barlow: a chauffeur drives a permanent secretary to and fro: both complain
of stomach ulcers, the permanent secretary as a result of eating too
much, the chauffeur because of an inadequate diet. It is a mood also captured
in John Ruganda's neat little poem about the fly-whisk so often used in
political rallies:

Fling it sharply, and growl:
Rebels hide their heads
Wave it gently, and smile:
Flies flit from pus drooping eyes
Sling it on the arm, finally:
Empty stomachs will drum for you.[9]

All this points to a very exciting, concerned literary output from East
Africa. Certainly, here is no literary desert.

REFERENCES

1 A talk given at the Institute of African Studies, University of Ghana.
  September 1969.
2 Ngugi, Owuor-Anyumba, Taban Lo Liyong: 'On the Abolition of the
  English Department', Faculty of Arts Nairobi (See Appendix).
3 Okello Oculi: *Prostitute* (East African Publishing House, Nairobi, 1968),
  p. 117.
4 Jonathan Kariara: *A Leopard Lives in a Muu Tree* (included in *Poems
  from East Africa*, eds. David Cook & David Rubadiri; Heinemann,
  London, 1971)
5 David Rubadiri: *Stanley Meets Mutesa* (included in *A Book of African
  Verse*, eds. John Reed and Clive Wake; Heinemann, London, 1964).
6 Okot p'Bitek: *Song of Lawino* (East African Publishing House, Nairobi,
  1967), p. 21.
7 *Song of Lawino*, pp. 188–189.
8 *Song of Lawino*, p. 196.
9 John Ruganda, *(Uka*, Vol. I, no. 1).

Part Three: Writers from the Caribbean

A Kind of Homecoming[1]

▼▼▼▼▼▼▼▼▼▼▼▼▼▼▼▼▼▼▼▼▼▼▼▼▼▼▼▼▼▼▼▼

We might as well start with a question. Should we study Caribbean literature in our schools and in our University colleges? For me there can only be one answer. I first came into contact with West Indian literature in English by a chance encounter with George Lamming's novel *In the Castle of My Skin*. He evoked through a child's growing awareness a tremendous picture of the awakening collective social consciousness of a small village. He evoked, for me, an unforgettable picture of a peasant revolt in a white-dominated world. And suddenly I knew a novel could be made to speak to me, could, with a compelling urgency, touch chords deep down in me. His world was not as strange to me as that of Fielding, Defoe, Smollett, Jane Austen, George Eliot, Dickens, D. H. Lawrence. That was in 1961.

On looking back I am amazed by our utter neglect of Caribbean studies in our Departments of Literature. How can we ignore the most exciting literary outbursts in the world today? We forget, or have been made to forget by our literary midwives from Britain, that the West Indies has been very formative in Africa's political and literary consciousness: Marcus Garvey, C. L. R. James, George Padmore, Aimé Césaire, Frantz Fanon: these are some of the most familiar names in Africa. Yet we ignore their work.

There is another bond, quite apart from such individuals' influence on African history. Africa, remember, was the dramatic scene of the cruel and bloody origin of the modern West Indies, the beginning of the islands' violent progress through what Eric Williams called 'the broiling sun of the sugar, tobacco and cotton plantation'. European greed, the motive force in capitalism, was not satisfied with merely physically wrenching a whole people from their mother continent, but further stifled any possibility of a continuous culture on the part of the captives by denying them a family life. Denied language and a common culture, deprived of political and economic power, and without the corrective of an unbiased, and all-sided, educational system even after 'freedom' was regained, the uprooted

black population looked to the white world for a pattern of life. C. L. R.
James in *The Black Jacobins* has spoken of this:

> The West Indies has never been a traditional colonial territory with
> clearly distinguished economic and political relations between two
> different cultures. Native culture there was none. The Aboriginal
> Amerindian civilisation had been destroyed. Every succeeding year, there-
> fore, saw the labouring population, slave or free, incorporating into itself
> more and more of the language, customs, aims and outlook of its masters.[2]

To Africa, to their past, even to their skin colour, they were made to look
in shame and discomfort. So that the West Indian intellectuals and writers
in between the Wars and even after may well have realized, as James has
said, 'that before they could begin to see themselves as a free and independent people they had to clear from their minds the stigma that anything
African was inherently inferior and degraded'. Hence their political, literary
and emotional involvement with Africa.

This involvement is often very real, and very personal. A few days after
arriving in Africa, E. R. Braithwaite, a Guyanese writer, underwent a
small but significant crisis:

> Here I was in Africa, but what was an African? Did the years of slavery
> and manumission through which my forbears passed completely separate
> me from these people? Was there part of me which remained African
> after all these years?[3]

Later he gave up the struggle to find a particular point of origin and
embraced the whole continent. 'Perhaps I am lucky,' he wrote in *A
Kind of Homecoming*, 'in that I have no known point of origin; all Africa
is therefore my original home, and I am at liberty to make it my
home.'

Yet there has been a lot of argument over the African presence in the
Black West Indian consciousness. V. S. Naipaul has argued that despite
the twenty millions who made the middle passage, scarcely an African
name remained in the New World. 'Until the other day,' he wrote in
Middle Passage, 'African tribesmen on the screen excited derisive West
Indian laughter.' Naipaul's comments were slightly exaggerated. There
have been, according to O. R. Dathorne, genuine African cultural survivals
in names of certain foods and in the practice of various religious cults in
Haiti, Jamaica, and Trinidad. 'It is precisely because Africa has not been
forgotten,' wrote George Lamming in reply to V. S. Naipaul, 'that the

West Indian embarrassment takes the form of derisive laughter.' The surprising thing in fact is that despite the years of lies and distortion about Africa, the African consciousness should still form such an important element in West Indian awareness. This is borne out by the centrality of Africa in a lot of West Indian fiction. The debate about Africa's presence in the West Indian consciousness is, for instance, central to Andrew Salkey's first novel *A Quality of Violence*. A drought in the village has precipitated the crisis in the novel. What action they should take is one of the divisive contentions among the peasantry. In reality the drought has only revealed the hidden forces in each individual: but how they should interpret the African image is important in the ensuing struggle over men's souls and over the social direction of the whole community. One faction denies the African presence (in their blood).

> We is people who live on the land in St. Thomas, not Africa. You hear? We is no slave people, and there is no Africa in we blood the way you would-a like we to believe.

The other holds a contrary view:

> Everybody is a part of slavery days, is a part of the climate-a-Africa and the feelings in the heart is Africa feelings that beating there, far down . . . We all come down from Ashanti people who did powerful plenty, and we have the same bad feelings that them did have.[4]

Some writers, after visiting the continent (or after living there for a time), have even set their novels in a physical Africa. The main theme in such novels is a search for roots through a personal involvement with actual Africa. The main hero, as in Denis Williams' novel *Other Leopards*, is depicted as going to Africa in search of another person, a symbolic man synonymous in Williams' case with 'this other ego of ancestral times that I was sure slumbered behind the cultivated mask'. *Other Leopards* is set in the Sudan. The hero's estrangement from his world and himself starts with a discomfort with his Christian (white) name, Lionel: he wants to find more about the other (African) name, Lobo, which his sister had once given him.

> She called me Lobo, and Lobo I became, except that Lionel remained on my birth certificate and is set to plague me like a festering conscience for the rest of my days, look of it. I became Lobo and that's the whole trouble; I am a man, you see, plagued by these two names, and this is

their history; Lionel, the who I was, dealing with Lobo, the who I continually felt I ought to become.[5]

He identifies Lobo with the primitive, instinctual man – 'the one I carried like a pregnant load waiting to be freed – to roam back to the swamps and forests and to the vaguely felt darkness of my South American home.'

Lionel Frond's dichotomy is similar to what also ails Dathorne's hero in *The Scholar Man*. Adam Questus goes to Africa in search of an unidentified Egor, with whom he had spent eighteen primitively happy years in the West Indies. Adam Questus is really in search of a lost identity: in the plane he can even feel 'the slave blood in his veins that made him somehow part of the whole of Africa'. Talking to the daughter of the head of the department at the West African university where he teaches, Adam Questus spells out the nature of his quest:

'I'm of African parents who emigrated to the West Indies. I was brought up there.' He stopped. He remembered Egor. She looked at him coolly while he talked. She took a cigarette. He lit it.

'Go on,' she said. 'Please bare your soul. I adore spiritual nakedness – it's more decent.'

(It was becoming increasingly difficult for him to clothe his thoughts in words.)

'As a person who has grown up from my past I don't know any thing about myself. I know all I'm not. I am not English. I suppose I'm not even really West Indian.'

She blew out a cloud of smoke.

'And so,' she said, 'our hero has come to West Africa to discover himself.'

'No,' he answered a little ruefully, 'I haven't plagiarized that from the modern mania for discovering oneself. But try to understand. I do want to know what's what – where I belong.'[6]

Although both Dathorne and Williams have lived in Africa and their novels are set in the contemporary scene, their Africa feels unreal, sometimes weird. There is greater realism in Williams' novel, and this helps to make the hero's spiritual predicament and its uneasy resolution credible. But Dathorne's Africa is unrecognizable: it is full of witch-doctors who find themselves invited to international scientific gatherings, immigration authorities who compose pompous letters merely to complain that an apple, a single apple, has been illegally brought into the country, and effeminate, imbecile students who spend their time analysing the political symbolism of Baa Baa Black Sheep. Both Dathorne and Williams are not, of course, concerned with the African situation: they are more interested in their hero's central quest, and use physical Africa as a symbolic backcloth.

In the novels of Sylvia Wynter and Orlando Patterson we do not get a physical Africa. With them Africa is a symbol with which West Indian semi-religious organizations identify themselves in their rejection of Christian-colonial values and the living conditions around them. The stinking poverty is a physical presence which more than the cultural-spiritual dichotomy of Williams' and Dathorne's heroes alienates the West Indian working class, exiled as they are in slum ghettos. In *The Hills of Hebron*, Sylvia Wynter depicts Cockpit Centre as an Egypt of stinking narrow streets, concrete sidewalks that burn one's feet and gutters gushing with dirty water.

> At nights the street-lamps cast arcs of murky light on the shops, the houses, the churches, the shacks crowded together in grey slums, the bunched figures sleeping on the pavement, on benches, in the park, but huddled together, secure in their acceptance of the ordinariness of hunger, poverty and defeat.[7]

These are the conditions that breed despairing men who turn to religion as a last hope for a social cure. Moses Barton sees himself as a prophet chosen by 'the God of the black men, of the oppressed', and wants to create a kingdom of plenty on earth so that 'black men would no longer be strangers to their God. His image would now reflect theirs, and they would see themselves without self-doubt, self-hatred, self-mockery.' The same conditions breed men who have lost faith in any organized political revolt or creative association to struggle against social ills: they believe that their salvation lies in a flight to Africa. Thus a bearded Rastafarian, after being arrested, kneels down in a police van, fervently chanting:

> Ethiopia, awaken and hear thy children's cry,
> Ethiopia now is free, our cry rings o'er the land,
> Ethiopia awaken, the morning is at hand![8]

In *The Hills of Hebron*, identity with the African image is seen as a negative response to the festering sores plaguing West Indian workers. But Orlando Patterson, in *The Children of Sisyphus*, sees a similar identity as a necessary psychological prop in the struggle of the socially betrayed to remain human. Like garbage, the poor in Jamaica have been dumped in a slum town known as the Dungle.

This is where garbage is also dumped: the novel opens with three garbage men working their donkeys to death, and the whole scene reeks with cruel despair; people have been turned into animals.

> Every moment was a desperate step uphill, every movement of his shovel in the filth was a despairing surge of will, every glance of their eyes a terrifying punch of humiliation. He could only seek to forget by grasping frantically upon every incident, every object that would mercifully hide him from the consciousness of the moment . . . He had to forget. He would tell himself that he would not face them again. It was all a façade, anyway. All a meaningless, ghastly façade. And so it didn't matter what he convinced himself to believe. They weren't there. Those things. Those creatures of the Dungle. No, they weren't human. If anyone told him that they were human like himself he would tell them that they lied. Those eyes peering at him. Deep and dark red and hungry for what he carried. And for his own blood, too, he was sure. No, he had to forget. Only by forgetting could he possibly bear the burden of the moment . . .[9]

The novel depicts the attempts of various characters to climb out of the garbage society into which they were born. The Rastafarian movement is one of the organizations helping the wretched of the earth to rise above the absurdity of their situation. Brother Solomon, their leader, is seen as the reincarnation of Marcus Garvey – 'that champion of the negro race who had felt the vile wrath of the white man for his just and wise teaching' – and as the Black Moses who is really the embodiment of the spirit of Haile Selassie. A lot of Solomon's followers look to this African king for deliverance.

> De black god of we, de true Children of Israel, descendants of de black King Solomon an' de black Queen Sheba, they shall burn up de white dogs an' de brown traitors fo' pollutin' we woman wid dem evil ways.[10]

But Brother Solomon is portrayed as a leader with complex ideas: a return to Africa, he knows, is too simple a solution. He rejects Christianity, which he sees as both an opium of those oppressed and also as the major cause of human alienation:

> Yes, me Brother. But there is another thing they hide from us. The most important of all. And that is that man is God. The spirit of Rastafari is invested in every one of us. Is just for we find it. This, this, Brother,

is the wickedest sin that the white man commit on himself and us and that the brown allies now perpetuate.[11]

He sees imperialism as the enemy of all men, black and white.

It enslave the whiteman long time. It enslave the brown lackeys and the black traitors long time. And it keep us in perpetual damnation, Brother. It's our sweat that made England. It's our poverty it smothering over now. An' what this all mean, Brother? It mean that the God that is within you is locked up in the filthiness of poverty.[12]

In *Children of Sisyphus*, Africa is used as a symbol around which those who reject degradation cluster.

In *Land of the Living*, John Hearne has also explored the meaning of the African image as preached by the sons of Sheba. But the exploration is removed from the social realism of Patterson and Sylvia Wynter onto a mystical plane. Marcus Heneky, the leader of the Pure Church of Africa, is raised from the murky social conditions that create his kind up to the grandeur of myth. He is really a member of the agricultural middle class that people his novels, but this time dressed in a worker's garb. His very dwelling place, we are told, is very much like any other small settler's house.

But on the walls . . . there was a large photograph of the Ethiopian Emperor, with two green, yellow and red flags above the frame, their sticks crossed, the cloth spread flat, and a loudly coloured relief map of Africa on which Addis Ababa was symbolized by a huge, gilt star of David. On the third wall, facing this, was a framed text in twelve point Baskerville: *For the hurt of my people am I hurt; I am black; astonishment hath taken hold on me*.[13]

Heneky's physical presence has a charismatic appeal to those present, and even after his death he is a centre of controversy.

'He was,' I said. 'It's not easy to put into words, but when you knew him you felt it.'
'Felt what?'
'A sense of purpose. Choice maybe. You know, there are some men who feel that the pain of this world is one pain. Who try to assume it, struggle with it and free us from it. Marcus Haneky was like that.'
'God Almighty,' Oliver said, 'you Germans are all the same. Jew or

Gentile, you're all romantic. Look, Heneky had one idea and he limited
it to one race. Africa triumphant. You can agree he had a lot of justification for feeling the way he did, but no more. He felt that the turn of
the black man had come round. The only thing that I still haven't got
clearly is the man himself. What made him, unique, I mean.'

'That's what I'm trying to tell you,' I said. 'The triumph of Africa
and the black race was only the external part of it. A . . . a sort of symp-
tom. He wasn't just a common little fanatic, for all his limitations. I tell
you: that old man belonged in another class altogether. Perhaps he
didn't even know what moved him or what he was really trying to do,
but it was there all the same: the necessity to erase another bit of the
lie that makes slaves of us.'

'I've lost you,' Andrew said. 'What lie?'

'It all depends,' I said. 'It varies from time to time and place to place.
In Heneky's case the lie was that the black man was faceless. What he
had to do was try to change that, to give the black man the sort of vision
of himself that would make him free. And make the whites and the
browns free, because they were shackled to the lie too. But it wasn't just
a matter of giving the black man a vote, or ministerial portfolio, or an
equal income. All those things come into it, but there is something else
needed.'

'What?'

'A territory the heart can occupy.'

'You mean, you think that he was right in all that back to Africa
nonsense?'

'Not right in your terms, Andrew. Not in your politician's terms. But
true. A truth of passion . . .'[14]

A truth of passion! That is what connects Marcus Heneky with Hearne's
other heroes – Roy in *Stranger at the Gate*, or Jojo Rygin in *The Faces of
Love*. They are conceived as bundles of powerful passions shattering the
accepted order of things, tearing and exposing the thin veneer of civilization
covering the modern middle class. Hearne's heroes, even when affirming
an undefined truth and order, are seen as embodying a 'purposeless and
indescribable spirit of destruction'. But is this outside the explained conflicts
of race, class or commerce? The novel seems to imply so, and hence Marcus
Heneky is conceived as being in pursuit of something which somehow
cannot be explained in social terms. And that is why for all his heroic
grandeur Heneky remains a shadowy figure. This is not helped by the
self-consciously smooth romantic rhetoric of Hearne's narrator, who
attempts to extract universal applications from every episode and encounter.

The conditions that give rise to Rastafarians and such religious cults are neither romantic nor mysterious. But in *Land of the Living* immediate social reality is minimized: Heneky's search is lifted from its concrete social setting to a beautiful metaphysical plane. But the theme explored, i.e. the search for a territory the heart can occupy, is certainly central in West Indian fiction, however different the treatment and even degree of success.

The exploration of the African consciousness is part, a very important part, of that larger theme: the search for an identity in an essentially colonial situation: 'Who are we, where do we come from; and where do we go from here?'

Most characters in West Indian fiction, even in novels that do not specifically explore the African symbol, feel themselves estranged from their roots. They are haunted by a sense of unsettledness similar, in a way, to that of the Jews.

In fact there is something about the Jewish experience – the biblical experience – which appeals to the West Indian novelist. Biblical man has been a slave and an exile from home. In his pastoral rootless wandering in search of home, he lives closer to God and contends with the unpredictable caprice of natural forces. He has been persecuted, and because of his suffering he has attained a wisdom which gives him strength to await his deliverance and his return home from exile. He lives by hope, hope so close to certainty that it forms the basis of his passive resistance, his active rebellion against captivity.

One or a combination of these elements is frequently found in those writers who see a parallel between the West Indian and the Jewish biblical experience. Lamming's peasants, for instance, often resort to biblical mythology for a frame of reference and comparison. They live close to God and contend with treacherous fires and floods. The main character in Sylvia Wynter's *The Hills of Hebron* re-enacts the story of Moses and of Christ's crucifixion. Patterson's Rastafarians see themselves as black Israelites enslaved by the white man in Babylon. 'When shall Babylon fall,' they cry in their revolt against the slum city, 'when shall the oppressors suffer at the hands of the conquering lion of the Tribe of Judah for their wickedness?'

The overwhelming sense of exile in a white-dominated world drives Heneky to declare: 'our past he abandoned in Africa'. The words are echoed by Alexander Blackman, the main character in Patterson's novel *An Absence of Ruins*, when he claims to stand 'outside of race, outside of history, outside of any value'. Alexander Blackman is an intellectual. In fact, he scorns the idea of 'my golden Africa with its empires'. But it is one of those cultists who comes nearest to engaging his stone heart.

'We are all Jews lost in the wilderness, brother, and we are all black men, according to the Word. And the Word, which is the Truth, say unto I: In this world, in this life, every man is a Jew searching for his Zion; every man is a black man lost in a white world of grief.'[15]

This seems to be the theme of the novel. Alexander Blackman is possessed by a Sartrean nausea which arrests him in action or drives him to do the exact opposite of what he most desires. What ails him however is not a true existential anguish but the absence of a cultural stream to which he is heir. Thus in England he is envious of an English girl who seems completely immersed in her own culture: 'She was completely Anglo-Saxon, rooted in a past that was painstakingly obvious, totally involved in a culture that was every inch her own. I lacked not only the substance of such experiences, but even their form.' His spiritual ague is the old demon that drives Adam Questus and Lionel Frond in search of their egos in Africa.

What however makes the novel haunt one's memory is a sense of permanent emptiness – 'a kind of rush into emptiness, yet the very rush, the very surge, was itself an emptiness' – which the author manages to capture in the language he uses. The use of language to capture this sense of vacuum is the strong link between *An Absence of Ruins* and Naipaul's novel *The Mimic Men*. Underlying *The Mimic Men* is the same idea of emptiness and apparent futility of action: 'We could not obliterate the feeling of failure, the feeling of the house's emptiness, the feeling that whatever solution we achieved would be only temporary.' Success is momentary; involvement in action does not bring fulfilment but an empty feeling and a desire for yet another palliative. Both Singh and Blackman have been students in London. They return home, engage in politics for a time and then return to London, the city of disorder, to lose themselves, permanent exiles. Blackman is haunted by the absurdity of life, Singh by its comedy. Patterson's hero however remains too much his serious self. Naipaul's narrative tone is ironic, which makes him appear detached from his creation. Singh's predicament is bound up with wider but contemporary and historically actual issues of the breaking up of colonial empires and the operation of political power in the new states, and these are linked with the problem of order and disorder in the universe.

The pace of colonial events is quick, the turnover of leaders rapid. I have already been forgotten; and I know that the people who supplanted me are themselves about to be supplanted. My career is by no means unusual. It falls into the pattern. The career of the colonial politician is short and ends brutally. We lack order. Above all, we lack power, and we do not understand that we lack power. We mistake words and the acclamation of words for power; as soon as our bluff is called we are lost. Politics for us are a do-or-die, once-for-all charge . . . Our transitional or makeshift societies do not cushion us. There are no universities or City houses to refresh us and absorb us after the heat of battle. For those who lose, and nearly everyone loses, there is only one course: flight. Flight to the greater disorder, the final emptiness: London and the home counties.[16]

The image of the shipwreck – 'this feeling of being adrift' – stands astride the novel, a colossus of loneliness amidst disorder. Singh's career seems one vain effort to escape the shipwreck, and he ends up in London like Alexander Blackman mourning his state of alienation.

Both Singh and Alexander Blackman are intellectuals. Roger Mais, who wrote his books before Naipaul and Patterson, depicts an alienated individual and an alienated community of a different order and class. In *Black Lightning* the alienated individual is Jake, an artist-blacksmith in a self-contained rural community, who wants to assert the independence of the individual human being through his carving. The thought that if he were weak and helpless he would need somebody stronger on whom to lean fills him with resentment and bitterness. The fear of being dependent breaks his marriage and it drives him more and more into his carving of Samson, in which he wants to express his conception of human freedom. But he succeeds in depicting the contrary: his Samson, weighed with the burden he has to bear, leans forward a little, and his hand is resting on a little child.

'Look, Amos, if you could gather up all the suffering there is in the world . . . of all the folks who had lost their way in some kind of darkness, and of all who have known any kind of lack that human flesh and spirit can know . . . take all that suffering, and add it up . . . you would get something like that – that hopeless, uneven slump of the shoulders, that face.'[17]

The individual cannot live alone; Jake discovers this through his carving but also through his forced dependence on Amos once he is struck blind by lightning. He ends his own life. Jake refuses to accept that man is a composite of strength and weakness, independence and dependence. But Jake is alone not because he is an egocentric individualist seeing little in man, but because he can see so much: what really moves him is the helplessness of an individual in face of so much unrelieved suffering. Such suffering is the lot of the rejected community of Mais' two proletarian novels: *The Hills Were Rejoicing Together* and *Brother Man*. The community of *The Hills* live in a slum area – the Yard – from which none can escape. The prison where most of them go in and come out all their lives is an appropriate image. But the novel tells of the people's refusal to succumb completely to the criminal existence to which they have been condemned. Surjis's courage, untarnished by the misery around, and his equally uncorrupted love for Rema are an assertion of human dignity in struggle, a central assertion which is reinforced by the people's communal moments of joy and careless merriment. *Brother Man* tells of a similar struggle; but now the struggle is more obviously organized around a Christ-like figure who in trying to save the community becomes the object of scorn and violence. Both novels are full of brutal, animal violence. *The Hills* ends on a note of apparent defeat: Surjis's attempt to escape from prison is foiled by a single rifle-shot just at the moment when he is about to grasp at freedom: 'he hung suspended another instant, and then he seemed just to let go all he had won so desperately.' But *Brother Man* ends on a triumphant note: the Black Christ with only two faithful followers stands at the window and undergoes a kind of transfiguration: 'His heart was too full to speak. He saw all that lay before him in a vision of certitude, and he was alone no longer.'

Mais' characters are not articulate about their alienation, like those of John Hearne, Naipaul and Patterson. His characters are deformed by immediate social conditions. Their alienation is rendered in terms of the physical details of their daily celebrations of victory and defeat. We see their isolation and desolation so clearly, immediately, and precisely because these are not rendered in the abstract language of intellectual and spiritual introspection, as in *Land of the Living*, *The Mimic Men* and *An Absence of Ruins*, but to borrow a phrase from William Barrett's book *Irrational Man*, 'in the most powerful cry of the physical'.

What, however, is common to *Land of the Living*, *The Mimic Men*, *An Absence of Ruins* and Mais' novels is not only this sense of abandonment, dereliction and chaos but also a desire for the restoration of self. Marcus Heneky sees his role as redeeming his people's misshapen souls; Alexander Blackman is possessed by a longing for connection. Brother Man is a redeemer who in Jamaica's garden of Gethsemane takes on himself the sins that tend to dehumanize his fellow men: social frustrations, violence, and despair. Singh stops at what he calls his arrival at the bigger truth – a vision of chaos.

In a society like ours, fragmented, inorganic, no link between man and landscape, a society not held together by common interests, there was no true internal source of power, and no power was real which did not come from the outside. Such was the controlled chaos we had, with such enthusiasm, brought upon ourselves.[18]

But this is also a statement of what is needed before the restoration of order: an identity that holds things and society together.

The search for order and identity is the theme of Naipaul's major work, *A House for Mr Biswas*. The novel was written and published before *The Mimic Men*: but Mr Biswas' (peasant) struggle and optimism are the answer to Singh's (middle-class) despair. Like Singh, Mr Biswas is preyed upon by an all-pervasive sense of insecurity. As soon as his father dies, Mr Biswas and the family are driven into a Trinidadian wilderness – living with a penniless mother in one room of a mud hut. He is haunted by fear of the future.

> The future wasn't the next day or the next week or even the next year, times within his comprehension and therefore without dread. The future he feared could not be thought of in terms of time. It was a blankness, a void like those in dreams, into which, past, tomorrow and next year, he was falling.[19]

The disorder he dreads is symbolized by the House of the Tulsis, where they try to turn Mr Biswas into an object, to deny him private life and human individuality. These fears follow him into his forties so that his complexion grows dark, 'a darkness that seemed to come from within as though the skin was a murky but transparent film and the flesh below it had been bruised and become diseased and its corruption was rising.'

Mr Biswas is insecure in his 'home', insecure with his wife and children (who don't show him any loyalty) and insecure in his job, and with age creeping up on him, he is not even sure of his body.

But Mr Biswas does not merely contemplate the chaos. In the House of the Tulsis, he fights back. Invectives, with or without humour, tumble out with effortless ease. He weaves fantasies around himself. And when weak or cornered, he turns into a clowning comedian. Through comedy and fantasy he struggles to assert himself, his human identity. But beyond this, he struggles to anchor himself in something he can call his own. A house becomes the symbol for everything that life has denied him: it is a symbol of the order he wants to create. His triumph over chaos comes when at last he buys a house. The sense of belonging, of being rooted into his own, counterpoises, albeit uneasily, the overwhelming sense of exile and loneliness that has stalked his efforts in life:

He was struck again and again by the wonder of being in his own house, the audacity of it: to walk in through his own front gate, to bar entry to whoever he wished, to close his doors and windows every night, to hear no noises except those of his family, to wander freely from room to room and about his yard, instead of being condemned, as before, to retire the moment he got home to the crowded room in one or the other of Mrs Tulsi's houses . . . As a boy he had moved from one house of strangers to another; and since his marriage he felt he had lived nowhere but in the houses of the Tulsis . . . And now at the end he found himself in his own house on his own half-lot of land, his own portion of the earth. That he should have been responsible for this seemed to him, in these last months, stupendous.[20]

Mr Biswas' search for security and identity is seen in concrete, specific terms of a definite social struggle: throughout the novel, Naipaul never loses the concreteness of time and place and action. But we cannot help feeling that Mr Biswas is Caribbean man in search of himself and his place in the world.

This concern, this search for a connection, is not altogether alien to ourselves. The African Biswases, though shaped by a slightly different historical context, are involved in a similar task. Despite formal independence we live in an essentially colonial situation. The African masses, together with their West Indian counterparts, are still engaged in a social struggle which may, like Biswas' own struggle, end in a kind of homecoming.

REFERENCES

1 Talk given at Makerere University – September, 1968. Since then courses in Caribbean literature and even Black American literature are now being offered at Nairobi and Makerere Universities.
2 C. L. R. James: *The Black Jacobins* (reprinted Vintage Books, Random House, New York, 1963), p. 405.
3 E. R. Braithwaite: *A Kind of Homecoming* (Muller, London, 1963), p. 49.
4 Andrew Salkey: *A Quality of Violence* (New Authors Ltd, London, 1959), p. 151.
5 Denis Williams: *Other Leopards* (New Authors Ltd, London, 1963), p. 19.
6 O. R. Dathorne: *The Scholar Man* (Cassell, London, 1964), p. 48.
7 Sylvia Wynter: *The Hills of Hebron* (Cape, London, 1962), p. 26.
8 *The Hills of Hebron*, p. 271.
9 Orlando Patterson: *The Children of Sisyphus* (New Authors Ltd, London, 1964), p. 20.
10 *The Children of Sisyphus*, p. 46.
11 *The Children of Sisyphus*, p. 50.
12 *The Children of Sisyphus*, pp. 50–51.

13 John Hearne: *Land of the Living* (Faber & Faber, London, 1961), pp. 106–107.

14 John Hearne: *Land of the Living*, 109–110.

15 Orlando Patterson: *An Absence of Ruins* (Hutchinson, London, 1967), p. 96.

16 V. S. Naipaul: *The Mimic Men* (Deutsch, London, 1967), pp. 10–11.

17 Roger Mais: *Black Lightning* (Cape, London, 1955), p. 110.

18 V. S. Naipaul: *The Mimic Men*, p. 246.

19 V. S. Naipaul: *A House for Mr Biswas* (Deutsch, London, 1961).

20 V. S. Naipaul: *A House for Mr Biswas*, p. 8.

What is my Colour, What is my Race?

▼▼▼▼▼▼▼▼▼▼▼▼▼▼▼▼▼▼▼▼▼▼▼▼▼▼▼▼▼▼▼▼

The great Afro-American writer W. E. B. DuBois once voiced the prophetic words that the problem of the twentieth century was the problem of the colour line, 'the question as to how far the differences of race – which show themselves chiefly in the colour of the skin and the texture of the hair – will hereafter be made the basis of denying to over half the world the right of sharing to their utmost ability the opportunities and privileges of modern civilization.'[1] The question 'what is my colour, what is my race?' cannot really be ignored by black or non-white writers, especially those in a plural society. But whereas in America and South Africa this question has given rise to protest literature, in the 'British' West Indies even DuBois' moderate tone of protest is not to be found in their fiction. V. S. Naipaul at one time seemed to gloat over the fact that the West Indian novel is lacking in the stirring indignation found in Black American literature or in the race consciousness found in the negritude poetry of the 'French' West Indies and Haiti. In 1962, he wrote, with a sigh of relief one feels, that so far the West Indian writer had avoided the American Negro type of protest writing.

This was not an accident: it was in the very nature of the writers' background, the fact, for instance, that in the West Indies, unlike in America, the non-whites were always in the majority, the fact again that unlike in South Africa there never developed, in the post-emancipation West Indies, an openly repressive racist regime. More important though, and Naipaul himself provided the answer, was the type of education that the non-white received. Having been prepared by his education to believe himself heir to a Christian-hellenic tradition, Naipaul wrote, the West Indian (one presumes, of middle-class upbringing and aspirations) pursued the Western white culture without seriously doubting the rationality of its prejudices.[2] The British created a native middle class moulded on England without gloating about it like the French: the British assimilated her educated colonials most effectively without even paying the price, i.e. accepting them fully into British society with the inevitable result, as in the French case, of cultural and racial assertion. To inculcate someone with certain values without his realizing he has so been inculcated is the special achievement of the British ruling class. In the case of the West Indies, the British had, with a stroke of genius, lulled the serpent of race to sleep.

> It was only long years after that [C. L. R. James writes in *Beyond A Boundary*], that I understood the limitation on the spirit, vision and self-respect which was imposed on us by the fact that our masters, our curriculum, our code of morals, *everything* began from the basis that Britain was the source of all light and leading, and our business was to admire, wonder, imitate, learn; our criterion of success was to have succeeded in approaching that distant ideal – to attain it was, of course, impossible. Both masters and boys accepted it as in the very nature of things. The masters could not be offensive about it because they thought it was their function to do this, if they thought about it at all; and, as for me, it was the beacon that beckoned me on. The race question did not have to be agitated. It was there, But in our little Eden it never troubled us.[3]

It is interesting that Trumper in Lamming's *In the Castle of My Skin* discovers 'my people – the negro race' – only after he has visited America, where he listens to Paul Robeson singing 'Let My People Go', sees repressive white racialism and experiences mass political action. With his shattering experiences abroad, he returns to Barbados where, like James above, he finds that the confrontation between black and white is merely masked by clever British administrative tactics. But his eyes are now open.

> None o' you here on this islan' know what it mean to fin' race. An' the white people you have to deal with won't ever let you know. 'Tis a great thing 'bout the English, the know-how. If ever there wus a nation in creation that know how to do an' get thing do, 'tis the English. My friend in the States use to call them the administrators. In America I have seen as much as a man get kick down for askin' a question, a simple question. Not here. That couldn't ever happen here. We can talk here where we like if 'tis a public place, an' you've white teachers, an' we speak with white people at all times and in all places. My people here go to their homes an' all that. An' take the clubs, for example. There be clubs which you an' me can't go to, an' none o' my people here, no matter who they be, but they don't tell us we can't. They put up a sign, 'Members Only', knowing full well you ain't got no chance o' becomin' a member. An' although we know from the start why we can't go, we

got the consolation we can't 'cause we arn't members. In America they don't worry with that kind o' scatin' 'bout the bush.[4]

Trumper, as a character, really belongs to the West Indian novel of emigration.

In the novel, the West Indian writers are compelled to deal with black-white confrontation by the very nature of the situation. The West Indian emigrant finds himself grouped as a non-white, which means he is black. Often he finds himself discriminated against in jobs and in housing, or treated with deliberate rudeness in the ordinary round of social contact. When this happens the characters, even the gentle characters of Samuel Selvon, are made to voice bitterness close to that of a protest novel. Thus Galahad in Selvon's novel *The Lonely Londoners*, after nasty experiences involving his colour, complains:

Lord, what is it we people do in this world to have to suffer so? What is it we want that white people and them find it so hard to give? A little work, a little food, a little place to sleep. We not asking for the sun, or the moon. We only want to get by, we don't even want to get on.[5]

Even here, the protest is more of a sorry lamentation. Compare this with a similar outburst in Richard Wright's novel *Native Son*:

They hung up imaginary receivers and leaned against the wall and laughed. A street car rattled by. Bigger sighed and swore.
    'Goddammit!'
    'What's the matter?'
    'They don't let us do nothing.'
    'Who?'
    'The white folks.'
    'You talk like you just now finding out,' Gus said.
    'Never. But I just can't get used to it,' Bigger said. 'I swear to God I can't. I know I oughtn't think about it, but I can't help it. Every time I think about it I feel like somebody's poking a red hot iron down my throat. Goddammit, look! We black and they white. They got things and we ain't. They do things and we can't. It's just like living in jail. Half the time I feel like I'm on the outside of the world peeping in through a knot-hole in fence . . .[6]

Bigger is obviously more bitter and defiant than Galahad. Bigger's mood is generated by the fact that he is being denied things in his own country – the repressive atmosphere is closer to the skin – while Galahad is an exile in foreign land. Although the West Indian emigrant novel shows how the West Indian's confrontation with the white world often shocks him into self-awareness as a member of a race group, the mood generated even in hard conditions of exile is not bitter protest but a desire to make contact, to hold a human dialogue across the colour-line. A character in Lamming's novel *The Emigrants* sums up the general mood.

> . . . take the English. My feelings for them wus no hate, not real hate, 'cause when I come to think of it, if they'd just show one sign of friendship, just a little sign of appreciation for people like me an' you who from the time we born, in school, we wus hearin' about them, if they could understand that and be different all the hate you talk about would disappear.[7]

The gentle mood pervading the West Indian writer's treatment of black-white confrontation is not confined to the novels set abroad. It is also the mood often found in the novels set at home, except, perhaps, in the case of Mittelholzer.

In Selvon's novel *Turn Again Tiger*, a sugar-cane labourer in Trinidad reluctantly becomes involved with the English wife of the supervisor. Tiger is self-educated and ambitious. He wants to transcend the limitations of a labourer's enslavement in sugar cane. But he is primarily in search of life and understanding. Walking in the country, among the sprouting plants, or merely sitting idly, pondering about mundane things, he finds that from nowhere, 'a sudden consciousness murmurs the music of a forgotten song, a rich phrase is evoked by a passing figure seen as a dream.'[8] Once, for instance, amidst a quarrel with his father, he starts puzzling out the secret of the growth and change from a baby with soft hands and soft skin to a man with hardened, coarsened skin, and sunken eyes, 'wrestling with life and sweating to earn bread to eat'. Suddenly he is filled with a tremendous reverent awe for his father, who has managed to survive the rigours of life to reach old age. But in the trial of strength that follows, he fights not as a son against his father but as one man against another. Tiger is meticulously portrayed as a man in harmony with himself (despite his philosophical worries) and with the fertile earth around him: he has a sharp enquiring intellect fortified by constant dives into Shakespeare, Plato, and Aristotle; he makes friends easily, he is respected in Five Rivers because he is generous at heart, and can read and write; and now, in the trial of strength with the father, he has emerged the physical victor.

This harmony is broken the moment he meets Doreen, naked,

sunbathing by the river. Suddenly confronted with the white presence, Tiger is assailed with self-doubt and with that inferiority common with people of his father's generation.

> His first reaction was to get away before he was seen – not silently, but run wildly, as in panic. There was danger here, his thoughts were jumbled as he tried to reason it out, flashing across the years to his childhood, keep off the white man's land, don't go near the overseer's house, turn your head away if you see the white man's wife. Such were the warnings of old men who in their youth had laboured in the fields and passed their experiences to their sons. [His father] in particular, Tiger knew, had a grovelling respect for the white man, and only rebelled peacefully, in the night over a pipe, muttering grumbles in his sleep.[9]

Tiger, who considers himself as belonging to a generation that can look straight at a white person, is shocked to find he has inherited the fear. He fights against it, but at the moment of crisis, he finds himself unable to live up to his chosen standard of conduct: when the woman shouts a greeting at him, unreasoning terror seizes him, and he runs away madly. This completely shatters his previous conception of himself. He wants a second chance to repair the broken image.

> All his mind cried to go back, to repair this damage to his dignity before it was too late. He actually took a few steps angrily, thoughts flying about in his head confusedly, but of one thing he was sure: he had made a mistake in fleeing. He had run away like a little boy, scared, because a white woman had called out to him. He, Tiger, who had his own house, who had a wife and a child, who worked with Americans during the war, who drank rum with men and discussed big things like Life and Death, who could read and write. Better if he had cringed, if he had bowed and stooped and blurted out good morning like some illiterate labourer and asked if there was something he could do. But to run away, to panic as if the devil were at his heels – for that there was no forgiveness.[10]

The encounter does not let loose a stream of hatred or protest against the white presence and injustice. Not that the condemnation of racial bigotry and arrogance is absent: some characters complain that no non-white can hold a responsible job; Tiger's father, who is practically in charge of the whole sugar estate, cannot be trusted with paying out money; and Robinson, the supervisor, is depicted as arrogant and condescending. But the condemnation of racial injustice is incidental, merely implied. What interests Selvon is Tiger's interior life. The encounter has initiated a stream of self-exploration. His self-esteem broken, his harmony disrupted, Tiger takes to excessive drinking and a melancholy but ruthless questioning of the underlying purpose of life. 'You study this, you study that, and in the end you hungry, in the end you wondering whether you going to meet Singh for a drink . . .' Perhaps old men who have lived life will give him the answer which Shakespeare, Plato and Aristotle – 'all of them fellers are dead' – have failed to yield. In the end he discovers that no man can prescribe a formula for another. The individual attains wisdom by actively participating in life. Tiger cannot exorcise Doreen (white presence) by wishing her away, or ignoring the attraction that lingers in the air when the two are together. Their second meeting by the river, not surprisingly, is seen in terms of a human wrestling with self. The old dragon of fear shows its head – his leg muscles are taut to spring and run – but he cannot resist what is an inevitable clash.

Hatred, fear, lust, fought in him, jumbled, his heart was going thud, thud and sweat ran down his face and over his lips and he licked them for the moisture and couldn't swallow.

She took a step forward, another. She was close to him. He held the cutlass tightly and said to himself that he would kill her. When he said that, it gave him courage: his grip tightened and he felt that if he had killed her everything would be all right after.

That was why he held her, to kill her. And when she held on too, straining against him and caressing the sweat on his skin, he was entirely unaware of it. He crushed her to him and they fell locked like wrestlers on dry bamboo leaves. The cause of every personal catastrophe was in his arms, and hatred and lust struggled equally in him. What he did was done blindly and vengefully and he never knew how it was with Doreen. What had tortured him had taken the form of her and that was what he had under him writhing and biting his arms and chest. She never cried out or made a sound but her body was trying like water to quench the rage and fury of his and several times she locked her lips against his, then turned away to clamp like a suction on other parts of his body. Tiger ripped the white cotton shirt off her shoulders and her breasts heaved at him. She was murmuring to him, words he didn't hear or care about: the sound came to him like a moaning. But now there was nothing to think about, all he had to do was fight and conquer, turn the force that was pulling him down against itself. It was as if the weeks had been built up for this day, day by day, piling up and up and now he had burst like a heavy rain-cloud and all the frustration and fears would be expelled: he wouldn't run away again, because he would shed this thing from him and it would go away and leave him in peace forever.[11]

The contact, then, restores Tiger to himself and to life. In the end, the ritual in the wood is seen as an integral part of Tiger's initiation to manhood. *Turn Again Tiger* is a novel of growth: things teeming from the earth; and men and women moving in rhythm with the circle of the seasons. The novel ends in a rather romantic universal harmony at harvesttime. Selvon's white characters are never central, they reside at the edges of the action. Their alien presence, however, does affect the peasant's and the worker's relations with his world. The peasant/worker's humour, and his dogged refusal to bow to hardship, makes him invincible by the destructive side of the white presence.

Selvon's gentleness and earthy warmth contrast with the violence of Edgar Mittelholzer. In the Kaywana trilogy[12], the master's lashes on the body of the slave, the throbbing sexual energy temporarily sweeping away barriers of race and even those between a mother and son, and the fearful possibilities of in-breeding and heredity, are all played out against what Dathorne has called the 'brooding landscape'[13] of the Guyana jungle. The trilogy goes back to the seventeenth century; through the fortunes of one family, Mittelholzer recreates the violent history of Guyana to the dawn of the twentieth century. The Von Groenwegels believe in the preservation of the strong blood. Their motto is never to surrender even if the whole world is pitted against them, a doctrine which is passed from parents to children: their mission in life is to nurture the strong streak in the family even at the expense of inbreeding. Hendriekje, a second-generation Groenwegel, perfects this outlook into a Nazi-like obsession with the power and purity of a master race of which she is the great grandmother. She argues that the stronger always survive and the weaker get crushed. Life is brutal. This is not pleasant, but a Von Groenwegel must face it as the truth. With such an obsession, a clash across the colour-line (which is also the dividing line between the slave and the master) is inevitable. And when it comes, it is full of relentless cruelty as the slaves, temporarily free, attempt to assuage a century of terror by punishing the white oppressor. The slaves, after capturing some white planters, make the women undress as a sign of submission.

When Amelia was naked, Cuffy grunted. He licked his lips, his gaze shifty. His head trembled. He paced about and then stopped and glared at Jacques. 'Von Groenwegel, you see your woman! Look at her! She standing with all her clothes off! Naked! You see how she hanging her head. She shame. Yes, she shame!'

His breath came in a strangled manner. He thrust his hands into his pockets and withdrew them again; they were trembling. 'Last week – before the twenty-first of this month – if I try to touch her skirt you white people give me twenty lashes and brand me on my chest. But now I is Governor! Your woman got to stand before me naked and do what I tell her to do. Georgie, get into bed! Go on! I orders you!'

Amelia stood where she was.

'Yes that hard for you to do. You never think one day come when you got to lie in bed with black man, eh, Georgie? But that what you got to do now.'

He moved toward her and halted. 'I got no mercy on you. I is Governor now. Yes, me Cuffy standing here. I is Governor, and you is my woman. You hear that, Von Groenwegel? From now she is my woman. And not just for lust – I want her. I want her so I can shame her – and shame her! Every day I going to shame her like how you white people shame our black women.' He put out his hand and fondled her breasts. His head trembled. He gulped. 'Yes, Georgie, I got to shame you so shame you you never want to look black man in the face again and think your-self better than him. Night and morning I going to shame you. You going to turn sick with shame.' He slapped her face. She was crying softly. 'Just for shaming you I going to shame you! Get into bed! Get in.' He spat in her face. 'Get in!'[14]

Jacques, who is in the room, asks to leave. He is one of the weak Groen-wegels because inwardly he does not share the hard iron outlook of his Grandmother Hendriekje. But Cuffy wants him to witness the act. He appeals to Cuffy's sense of decency. Cuffy is surprised that a white man, of all people, can ever expect a black man to show decency.

'I know it going to be hard for you to watch me and her in bed. But I glad it going to hurt you. I want to hurt you, Von Groenwegel. I been waiting years and years for this time when I can punish you Christians for the misery what you bring on us black men. I glad it going to give you pain. Sit down there on that chair and keep your eyes on the bed. Go on. Sit down – or else you go to the stocks!'[15]

Cuffy protests his ferocity a little bit too much. The slaves heap indignity on the white captive as much to convince themselves that they are now on top as to shame their erstwhile masters.

Mittelholzer remains detached where Selzon is involved with his peasant characters. But in both, the direct confrontation between white and black is rare, and there is little of race consciousness or racial assertion. This is because 'What is my colour, what is my race?' is more complex in the West Indies than in other settings.

Naipaul, in *Middle Passage*, has satirically described West Indian society as having divided people into 'white, fusty, musty, dusty, tea, coffee, cocoa, light black, dark black'. It is the colour problems and the values inherent in such a society which interest West Indian novelists: broad black-white encounter, even when it is prominent, is often seen as part of what Dathorne calls 'the polygenous races' that make up the West Indian scene. In *A Morning at the Office* one character castigates those who 'had purposely blinded themselves to the fact if the West Indies was to evolve a culture individually West Indian, it could only come out of the whole hotch-potch of racial and national elements of which West Indies is composed; it could not spring only from the Negro'.[16] And Dathorne argues that it is the way this hotch-potch of races intermingle in the West Indian novel that distinguishes it 'from the narrower dimensions of the standard European fiction'[17].

John Hearne's novels, for instance, are peopled with a cosmopolitan middle class: there is a European Jew who, in the islands, feels 'that some sort of obscure, powerful resurrection of myself has begun to stir'[18]. Englishmen with dreams of retirement in an England they were not born in and had only seen as visitors; Englishmen whose first intention is to stay in the islands long enough to acquire specialist knowledge but find the islands claiming them;[19] numerous characters (usually from the higher echelons of the professions and from the old landed gentry) of German, French, and African extraction whose one common denominator is their involvement with the islands. George Lamming also accepts the fundamental unity of the hotch-potch, but sees this unity more among the workers, peasants, and children. In *Of Age and Innocence*, he uses three children representing the three main racial extractions – African, Indian, Chinese – as a symbol of a West Indian community freed from the conflicts of race and colour. In *Pleasures of Exile* Lamming comments on the diversity of complexions of the three boys. 'They might have come from three different parts of the world. Yet they speak the same idiom, live the same history.' With his belief in the fundamental unity of the West Indian experience, he ridicules the West Indians, especially those who make the professional middle class and who place moral value on minute differences of skin colour. Two characters in *The Emigrants* – Miss Bis, who being 'one remove from the white' breaks her engagement to a West Indian doctor 'several shades darker than her', and Mr Dickson, who is utterly ashamed of his black skin – are the objects of the author's ridicule and slightly malicious satire. Selvon's different characters share a common experience of toil in English factories or of joyous struggle in the sugar-cane fields. They are only superficially sensitive to the different shades of colour; even then, they end up laughing at it or weaving ballads around it. Thus in *Turn Again Tiger*, Soylo, an Indian hermit, silences Otto's objections to marrying a black woman by warning him that were he to be choosy he would end up without a wife. He adds: 'Nigger and Chinese does make good children'. In *The Lonely Londoners*, the blackest character in the group is nicknamed 'Midnight'. But a new man joins the group and is christened 'Five-past-twelve'. V. S. Naipaul on the other hand isolates and explores the Indian community, maybe because he finds it has what he, quoting Graham Greene in *Middle Passage*, believes comedy needs: 'a strong framework of social convention with which the author sympathises but does not share'. In most of his novels, characters of African, Chinese or European origins flit about on the fringes of the action. But even in Naipaul, 'the delicacy of colour perception',[20] or what he himself describes as 'having a nice eye for shades of black' often governs or influences the pattern of human relations.

The subterranean corrosive effects of this – what yet another West Indian writer has called 'tint discrimination'[21] – are well examined and exposed in Mittelholzer's early novel, *A Morning at the Office*. With their different shades of colour and racial origins, people working for Essential Products Ltd. superficially make a harmonious cosmopolitan picture. But they are all trapped in their skins. There is Horace Xavier, an office boy with dreams of being the mayor of Port of Spain and a secret passion for the Manager's secretary; but he inwardly knows that his dark colour and his lowly position are in his way.

> He considered that it was foolish of him to have become enamoured of this lady. He was only a black boy, whereas she was a coloured lady of good family. His complexion was dark brown; hers was pale olive. His hair was kinky; hers was full of large waves and gleaming. He was a poor boy with hardly any education, the son of a cook; she was well off and of good education and good breeding. He was lowclass; she was middleclass.[22]

Nevertheless, the passion dominates him, filling him with 'uncertainty and instability' to such an extent that one morning he scribbles a few love lines from *As You Like It* and pushes the unsigned paper in her tray. Mr Jagbir, the Assistant Accountant and an East Indian, is another man plagued by a feeling of racial and personal inferiority. A labourer for four years after leaving school, Mr Jagbir 'had been cursed at and threatened and humiliated by a white overseer', which scarred him for life, so that at fifty, a father of four children, he believes that the white people are at any time liable to dismiss him from a job he has been doing for years.

> He made it his business to be well-informed concerning everything that went on in the office. His ears were perpetually on the alert, for the fear was always with him, that, despite his efficiency as a bookkeeper, he would one day be thrown out. He had been brought up to feel that an East Indian's place was in the field . . . shovelling and weeding. An office was meant for white people and good-class coloured people.[23]

The haunting insecurity drives him into sly, prying, but sycophantic habits which make people actually despise him. Their reaction only confirms his inner fears and he shrinks further into his infuriating defensive posture.

Even the privileged class of the whites and the good-class coloured are shown as equally trapped. Mr Murrain, the manager, though attracted to the accounts typist, a coloured girl, will not let himself go beyond his white skin.

> He tried to convince himself that he was above race and class prejudice, but the feeling of aloofness remained. The final conclusion would always be that he was distinctly on a higher level.[24]

Having little to do in the office his main passion is reading the gossip column of the *Trinidad Guardian* to see if he and his wife have been mentioned. Miss Henerey, the girl to whom he is attracted, belongs to that coloured middle class that conceive of human hair in terms of 'good' and 'bad', where 'good' stands for hair which is European in appearance. Conscious of her background of gentility and superiority over the negro, Chinese or Indian elements, she slightly resents the fact that the whites debar her from their society.

> But like everyone in her class she considered herself the equal of the whites in breeding and general culture. Her pride forbade her addressing a white man as 'Sir'.[25]

A clash between her and Mr Murrain, who resents her sauciness, is inevitable. It comes over her leave, to which she is legally entitled. But Mr Murrain is out to hurt her.

'But, Miss Henerey – really, sometimes I wonder if you forget that to your ancestors such a luxury as leave was entirely unheard of.'

'Which of my ancestors? Some were whites. Could you be referring by any chance to the English ones who were made slaves from childhood in the factories of 19th century industrial England?'[26]

Her quick retort makes him quickly retreat into the castle of his skin; but he cannot any more hide the loneliness under that white skin.

The awareness of human loneliness inevitably bred by such a society alleviates the often ill-disguised didacticisms of the novel. The description of Mr Reynolds, one of the very few positive characters in the novel, is an accurate epitaph on the interior state of the other characters.

He was afraid of himself. He dreaded introspecting, for when he introspected he pitied himself and saw his loneliness as a thing of magnified terror and ugliness – something that would pursue him to the end of his days.[27]

In this novel, Mittelholzer has portrayed the secret, psychic forces that govern people's inner thoughts in a society which has made minute differences of the skin the basis of morality and human relationship. Such a society alienates its human individuals and makes them live as exiles from themselves and from a country to which they rightly belong.

Even when such a society is calm on the surface, it quivers with a concealed violence, which occasionally erupts into a threatening force, as when a Rastafarian confronts a group of coloured students in Hearne's novel *Land of the Living*. The students, with their teacher, are on a biological excursion to a part of the island they have little frequented. Insulated by what the teacher-narrator describes as 'the academic ghetto of the university compound' the students have never met members of this semi-religious group, whose theme is a return to Africa, because as black men they see themselves as exiles. Hearne sees the Rastafarian as embodying elemental violence and describes him in terms of animal imagery. He is tall and lean, 'as a strayed domestic animal becomes gaunt and harsh on its foraging.' A tremendous tensed hardness, we are told, seems to 'radiate from that narrow body', and he speaks in 'an impersonal, waggish derision more corrosive than hate', while from 'the far back in the rough forest of shaggy beard, matted hair and heavy writhing brows' his eyes glare with a bleak, unwinking ferocity. The effect of his physical presence is to make everybody tremble 'on the edge of squalid violence', an effect strengthened by his voice and words.

An' I know how de white man want to eat up de children of Africa an'
hold dem in bondage . . . Dis land an' de whole eart' belong to de white
man, an' de black man is his slave. You come here fe' mek more plot
against we black. But our day come. Our God will come . . . Black an'
shinin' terrible . . . Africa's children will turn and rule.[28]

What many West Indian writers ignore is the economic basis of much of
this colour distinction. The black man, that is, the non-white, has suffered
both on the basis of his skin colour, and more fundamentally as one of the
class of exploited peasants and workers all over the world. Africa's children
(the non-whites) need to realize themselves on these two levels.

To create a religion of skin colour is to despair of a solution for social
injustice. But to ignore it is also dangerous. The West Indian black character will discover not only his colour and race, and claim them with pride,
but also his class – and seek solidarity with the exploited millions on the
islands and throughout the world.

REFERENCES

1 W. E. B. DuBois, *An ABC of Colour* (Berlin 1964), p. 20. The essay in
   question was an address he made to the Pan-African Conference in
   London, 1900.
2 V. S. Naipaul, *The Middle Passage* (Deutsch, London, 1962), p. 69.
3 C. L. R. James, *Beyond a Boundary* (Hutchinson, London, 1963),
   pp. 38–39.
4 George Lamming, *In the Castle of My Skin,* (McGraw-Hill, New York,
   1954), p. 303.
5 Samuel Selvon, *The Lonely Londoners* (Wingate, London, 1956), p. 89.
6 Richard Wright, *Native Son* (Signet Edition, New York 1964), pp. 22–23.
7 George Lamming, *The Emigrants* (Joseph, London, 1954), p. 186.
8 Samuel Selvon, *Turn Again Tiger* (MacGibbon & Kee, London, 1958),
   p. 13.
9 Samuel Selvon: *Turn Again Tiger*, p. 65.
10 Samuel Selvon: *Turn Again Tiger*, p. 65.
11 Samuel Selvon: *Turn Again Tiger*, p. 177.
12 Edgar Mittelholzer: *Children of Kaywana* (Peter Nevill, London, 1952
   and Secker & Warburg, London, 1956); *The Harrowing of Hubertus* (also
   called *Kaywana Stock*) (Secker & Warburg, London, 1954); *Kaywana
   Blood* (Secker & Warburg, London, 1958).
13 O. R. Dathorne: 'The Writers of Guyana', *Times Literary Supplement*,
   (May 6, 1966).
14 *Children of Kaywana*, p. 330.
15 *Children of Kaywana*, p. 331.
16 Mittelholzer, *A Morning at the Office* (Hogarth Press, London, 1950),
   p. 214.

17 O. R. Dathorne, *Caribbean Narrative* (Heinemann, London, 1966), p. 9.

18 John Hearne, *Land of the Living* (Faber & Faber, London, 1961), p. 13.

19 John Hearne, *The Faces of Love*, (Faber & Faber, London, 1957), p. 26.

20 Kenneth Ramchand: 'The Colour Problem at University', in *Disappointed Guests*, eds. H. Tajfel and J. Dawson (OUP, London, 1965), p. 29.

21 Elliot Boshen: 'The Weary Road to Whiteness', in *Disappointed Guests*, p. 42.

22 *A Morning at the Office*, p. 16.

23 *A Morning at the Office*, p. 27.

24 *A Morning at the Office*, p. 49.

25 *A Morning at the Office*, p. 48.

26 *A Morning at the Office*, p. 92.

27 *A Morning at the Office*, p. 175.

28 *Land of the Living*, p. 49.

George Lamming's
In the Castle of My Skin

▼▼▼▼▼▼▼▼▼▼▼▼▼▼▼▼▼▼▼▼▼▼▼▼▼▼▼▼▼▼▼▼▼▼

It will be our argument that although it is set in a village in a period well before any of the West Indian islands had achieved independence, *In the Castle of My Skin* is a study of a colonial revolt; that it shows the motive forces behind it and its development through three main stages: a static phase, then a phase of rebellion, ending in a phase of achievement and disillusionment with society poised on the edge of a new struggle; that it sharply delineates the opposition between the aspirations of the peasantry and those of the emergent native élite, an opposition which, masked in the second phase, becomes clear during the stage of apparent achievement. The novel itself is built on a three-tier time structure corresponding broadly to our three stages: the first three chapters describe stable life, a village community whose social consciousness is limited to a struggle with immediate nature; the next six chapters deal with a village whose consciousness is awakened into a wider vision, involving challenge of and struggle against the accepted order of things; while the last chapters show the ironic denouement; a new class of native lawyers, merchants, teachers has further displaced the peasantry from the land. But underlying the story's progress in time is a general conception of human history as a movement from the state of nature to a 'higher' consciousness; it is a movement from relative stability in a rural culture to a state of alienation, strife and uncertainty in the modern world.

The restless note is struck at the very beginning: looking at the rain, the hero can see the raindrops in terms of his inferior life: 'our lives – meaning our fears and their corresponding ideals – seemed to escape down an imaginary drain that was our future'.[1] The image anticipates the end, where the boy now about to embark on an adult's world away from home casts a last glance behind him:

> The earth where I walked was a marvel of blackness and I knew in a sense more deep than simple departure I had said farewell, farewell to the land. (p. 312.)

The words – note the finality and a wistful remembrance in the tone – sum up what has happened: not only the boy's childhood but an organic way of life has ended; the village has also embarked on an uncertain future. What is this organic life, and what are the forces disturbing it?

In the Castle of My Skin is, on the immediate level, the story of a boy's adolescence in a small peasant village in Barbados. It opens with the boy's ninth birthday, but straight away we are plunged into the recurring theme of loss.

> That evening I kept my eye on the crevices of our wasted roof where the colour of the shingles had turned to mourning black and waited for the weather to rehearse my wishes. But the evening settled on the slush of roads that dissolved parts into pools of clay, and I wept for the watery waste of my ninth important day. (p. 1.)

For nine years the rain has doggedly marred his birthday; flattery from the elders that his birthday has brought blessings is not adequate compensation. His awareness of loss, of absence, goes deeper than mere lack of sunny celebrations: his father has gone and left him in the charge of his mother; his grandfather is dead, and his grandmother gone to Panama.

> My birth began with an almost total absence of family relations, and loneliness from which had subsequently grown the consolation of freedom was the legacy with which my first year opened. (p. 3.)

Although, very occasionally, we encounter him among his young friends – Trumper, Boy Blue, Big Bam, Botsie, Knucker Hand, Po King, Puss in Boots, Suck me Toe – as they collect around the lamp posts, play at the seaside and go to school, he dwells in a private world, containing what Lamming elsewhere calls 'the range of his ambitions, his deceits, his pride, his shame, his guilt and his needs'.[2] This world, under the castle of his skin, is all-pervasive, especially in the early chapters of the book. Fear and insecurity pursue him into the night, when 'those phantoms that populated my brain came out to frighten me with the freedom which the night had brought them'. They dance and jeer 'through the thick black space of this narrow room'. Images of grime and dirt, wreckage, death reinforce the sense of permanent loss and deprivation. So we read of his birthday drifting outside in a fog of blackness that covered the land, of light leaking past frosty domes falling on water, of the poor who 'like their stalled beloved in the distant cemetery, sleep peacefully beneath the flying spray of rain', and of 'my birthday making its black departure from the land'.

But the boy's life is skilfully interwoven into his social and physical environment. His world is close to nature. Images of sea, earth, sky and wind abound: when a palm tree near the school sways left and right, the church steeple seems to listen 'as the wind carried their chorus across the village and into the sea'. On their way to sea, the boys are intimately aware of parakeets hopping from bark to bark, or screeching on tree-tops, of the sky collecting into a thick, white wave, apparently driven by a power external to it. He devotes large sections to painting nature:

The morning was now a clear indication of day. The parakeets' scream had died down or fused with other birds' carolling, and these were several. The sparrows chirped a quick, staccato cry that seemed more like an accident than an intention, while the blackbirds clawing the leaves made a strained high-pitched wail as mournful as the colour of their feathers. Only the doves seemed to have found some place in these surroundings. They were nearly all on the ground fluttering from pavement to the street and back, tripping along the hedgerows, leaping to the lower limbs of the trees, and diving back to the road. They paraded in thick squads on the tennis lawn. The brown bodies seemed to slope all together to meet the bluerigged necks and the heads that were neither round nor flat. The sun spotted them and they marched in circles over the lawn. The line was broken, but the movement was regular as they crossed the green turf from one end to the other, keeping time with their coos and carrying in their eyes all the colours of the rainbow. (pp. 108–109.)

Through his evocation of nature, he manages to capture a certain quality of life: almost as if there were harmony, a togetherness embracing man, beast, earth and sky. But nature can also be destructive. The boy himself is born into rain; his ninth birthday is a perennial birth into nature; floods with a potential power to change everything 'level the stature and even conceal the identity of the village'.

The white stalks of the lily lay flat under the hammering rain, then coaxed their roots from the earth and drifted across the upturned clay into the canals and onto the black deep river where by agreement the floods converged. The water rose higher and higher until the fern and flowers on the verandah were flooded. It came through the creases of the door, and expanded across the uncarpeted borders of the floor. My mother brought sacks that absorbed it quickly, but overhead the crevices of the roof were weeping rain, and surfacing the carpet, and the epergne of flowers and ferns were liquid, glittering curves which the mourning black of the shingles had bequeathed. No one seemed to notice how the room had passed to evening, the evening to night; nor to worry that the weather had played me false. Nothing mattered but the showers of blessing and eternal will of the water's source. And I might have accepted the consolation if it weren't that the floods had chosen to follow me in celebration of all my years, evoking the image of those legendary waters which had once risen to set a curse on the course of man. (pp. 1-2.)

The reference to Noah's flood and to biblical mythology throughout underlines the parallel between the experiences of Creighton village and those of a Hebrew pastoral peasant community. Only Creighton village is a small world in which 'a curious one way affection grew between the villager and the road he lived on' and often a mutual antipathy developed between the dwellers in one street and those in another. So like Synge's peasants, Creighton villagers love gossip and convert small events into stimulating legends. Thus the heavy rain and floods are not *any* water, but the second coming of Noah's flood; when Forster refuses to leave his house even at the risk of drowning, the incident is quickly handed from mouth to mouth and overnight passes into the village's popular mythology.

The water pour in through the floor boards till it reach his knee and then decide to go up on the roof. He climbs up and he and the house went sailing down the river while people shout out, 'Look, Noah on the Ark!'

This episode illustrates how the peasants are rooted to their world, and how much their house and plot of land means to them. Homes, gossip, daily chores are an integral part of their small world: note how their social vision is limited, does not go beyond the immediate street. But gradually, from this organic, rather static world, certain things begin to emerge with a clarity that indicates areas of past and present tension and lines of developing crisis.

The boy's social milieu is dominated by woman. Brought up by his mother, he cannot even remember his father, who had left 'me the sole liability of my mother'. Miss Forster has six children, three by a butcher, two by a baker, and one whose father is never mentioned. The situation has roots in slavery, now fanned by the economic necessity that compels men to seek their fortune in urban areas or even further afield in America or England. Unable to comprehend what is at the root of this social phenomenon, the boys think it is the stupidity of their mothers which drives men from home. The boys' feeling about the situation ranges from gratitude to hostility.

> THIRD BOY: . . . 'Tis funny the way it happens. You hear the talking, an' suddenly somebody say easy easy, daddy comin', and suddenly everything is like a black out for the ears. You don't hear anything at all. Not a sound but their father foot coming through the yard. An' it stay silent so till he go out again.
>
> FOURTH BOY: We can do without father if that is how they like. I do without mine alright. An' then too, if there aint no father in the house, you get the feeling you is the man in the place. It's good feeling when anybody like sanitary inspector or the police come in an' ask who is the man round here, an' you say, well there's only one man round here, an' 'tis me.
>
> FIRST BOY: I don't see much of my father, but my second brother father is good. He don't make no difference between us, me and my brother, 'cause he says we is both our mother children. How many fathers you got in your family? (p. 40.)

Faced with a situation in which fathers are either absent or merely peripheral to the household, mothers try to exert a 'paternal' authority on rebellious boys by constant threats and flogging. The contest of will and wit between sons and mothers is well captured in a comic scene in which Bob, hiding from his mother's flogging, later escapes in a sack by playing bear, a children's game, and passes, unmolested, in front of his unsuspecting mother and other laughing women. The attitude of mothers to their sons is a mixture of impatient harshness ('The children bring botheration to parents nowadays. Look what the other one make me do this morning, but let him hide. Night run till day catch him.') tempered with tender understanding and warm physical affection. 'When all is said and done,' the women argue, 'they is ours and we love them. Whatever we mothers say or do, nobody love them like we'.

The villagers, numbering about three thousand, live in what is, essentially, a feudal society. At the head of the Estate is Creighton, whose house appropriately stands on a hill, dominating all below it. The overseers, the police constables and the school teachers make the middle stratum. At the bottom of this social hierarchy are the peasants, who over the years have acquired customary rights to their homes and plots of land. They accept the social order as divinely willed and dwell under the shadow of Creighton's paternal benevolence. Wealth, law and police power have combined in varying degrees to enforce this acceptance, and produce in

the mind of the villagers the idea of the great; subservient complexes
govern their every response to and contact with Creighton. What distinguishes Creighton Estate from earlier forms of feudalism, more highly
stratified with corresponding duties and rights, is its colonial setting with
roots in slavery. The rights and duties are divinely willed by Creighton
and Great Britain. The very educational system deliberately aims at buttress-
ing the attitude of acceptance. The schools celebrate Empire Day, the
King's birthday; they sing the British national anthem and embrace the
English history and heritage as their own. When the parents are invited
for Empire Day their minds go back to the day 'Good Old England and Old
Little England' had embraced.[3] The school receives the inspector with all
the pomp and ceremony surrounding a monarch's visit. Assuming that
stock pose of stiff dignity so characteristic of colonial administrators, the
inspector declaims the doctrine of partnership:

> My dear boys and teachers, we are met once again to pay our respects
> to the memory of a great Queen. She was your Queen and my Queen
> and yours no less than mine. We're all subjects and partakers in the
> great design, the British Empire, and your loyalty to the Empire can be
> seen in the splendid performance which your school decorations and the
> discipline of these squads represent. (p. 30.)

'Pax Britannica' among the darker races of the earth has now assumed a
global character. It is the Second World War, Britain and her colonies
must march on to victory over Hitler and Mussolini. This is the historical
mission of the British Empire.

> The British Empire, you must remember, has always worked for the
> peace of the world. This was a job assigned to it by God, and if the
> Empire at any time has failed to bring about that peace it was due to
> events and causes beyond its control. (p. 31.)

The Inspector's real attitude to his partners in this great design is revealed
in the tone of his voice, and more explicitly in his last few words.

> I hope I shall start no jealousy among the schools in the island under
> my control if I say that such a display as I see here could not have been
> bettered by the lads at home. (p. 31.)

The yardstick is England. Everything that affects the tender minds of
children is geared towards veneration of England and the British throne.

The headmaster distributes pennies – 'a gift of the Queen' – and solemnly assures them

> You must all when you got to spend your penny think before you throw it away. Queen Victoria was a wise queen, and she would have you spend it wisely. (p. 31.)

As the boys have not been told the truth about their past. slavery and the slave trade are a jumble of bits and ends in their minds. The Queen, they have been taught, had freed them. In that case

> They must have been locked up in a kind of gaol. That's what it was, one boy said quickly. Most of them were locked up in gaol at the same time in the past. And it would appear that when this good and great queen came to the throne she ordered that those who weren't free should now become free.

The only history which they have been taught is that of Britain.

> They had read about the Battle of Hastings and William the Conqueror. That happened so many hundred years ago. And slavery was thousands of years before that. It was too far back for anyone to worry about teaching it as history. That's really why it wasn't taught. (p. 52.)

Lamming evokes the confusion in the minds of the boys as they puzzle out a phenomenon they can't understand. At times they don't even believe it happened, or else explain issues of freedom and slavery in terms of biblical mythology.

> We are slaves. We are slaves to these two. The Empire and the garden. And we are happy to be slaves. It isn't the same as being a prisoner. Nobody wants to be a prisoner. But it's different when you're a slave. When you're a slave of the Empire and the Garden at the same time, you're free to belong to both. And you can be free to be ashamed of not thinking enough about them. The more you think of them, the more you are ashamed. My mother who is a Sunday School teacher has explained it well. There's nothing for us to do, she tells me, but rejoice in our bondage. That is what she calls it. She doesn't say slave. She says bondage. When the time comes, we shall be taken out of the bondage of what she calls grace . . . salvation through grace. We're all going the garden again, free again, and especially those who here on earth belonged to the Empire.

The Queen's birthday and the whole educational apparatus at Groddeck's Boys School, then, is used to encourage the myth of Barbados being little England. The boys' restless minds find the evasive answer of the older people and the teachers inadequate. What is slavery? What is freedom? Curious, puzzled and pained, the boys turn to religion for an answer. The Christian view of man (Make me a captive Lord and then I shall be free) seems to offer a meaningful explanation. Since the boys belong to a new generation that has no direct experience of slavery, and yet have no book knowledge of their immediate past, they seek to find their roots in a general human predicament of sin, death, resurrection and salvation by grace. Even more important for our argument, we are shown how they see this grace as lying somewhere in the Empire. Imperialism and colonialism become sanctified by Christian grace. And all this seems to point in one direction: subservience and acceptance.

But Lamming shows how the seeds of crisis already exist within the present order. Fear and antagonism rule the relationships between people in different social scales. The landlord might at first appear a god whose eminence and dominance is not to be questioned: whenever his son, for instance, passes through the village, the peasants move back, and he gives the order. He makes no demands, or few, we are told, but merely accepts a privilege they offer. There may be a silent protest, but no one is really angry – 'acceptance is all'. True, but people's fear and hatred are turned, not against the landlord directly, but against his middlemen: the overseers and the constables. To the villagers the overseer is the enemy. And to the overseer, the villagers are the enemy, 'the low-down nigger people because they couldn't bear to see one of their kind get along without feeling envy and hate'. At least that is what he thinks is the motive force behind their occasional refusal to obey his orders. The overseer walks on a tightrope of fear and insecurity: his enemy, 'my people', might at any time do something which would arouse Creighton's wrath; his privileged position is in constant jeopardy because it depends on the unpredictable will of the white people. He and the constable and the schoolteacher are the forerunners of the colonial bourgeoisie who co-operate with the white man and even share the oppressor's view of the peasants and workers. Rejected in the social world of the white rulers and alienated from the masses by their jobs and education, they turn their frustration inward, against themselves, or else vent it on their own people.

If the low-down nigger people weren't what they are, the others couldn't say anything about us. Suspicion, distrust, hostility. These operated in every decision. You never can tell with my people. It was the language of the lawyers and doctors who had returned stamped like an envelope with what they called the culture of the Mother Country. (p. 19.)

And yet it is from the ranks of the élite, precisely because they are better placed to articulate their desires and discontent, that you get the leaders of the colonial revolt. In *In the Castle of My Skin* it is a dismissed school-teacher, Mr Slime, who exploits and directs the village's collective consciousness into an instrument of challenge and change.

In the process of change, Mr Slime functions as a catalyst which releases the developing conflicts in society. Like Marcus Garvey, who from the moment he came down 'an' tells us that the Lord ain't going to drop manna in we mouths I start to think', Mr Slime kindles in them a dream ('he speak the other night how he goin' to make us owners o' this land . . . I couldn't sort of catch my breath when I hear it, but 'tis a big thing to expect . . .'), which makes them look differently at the hitherto existing relations on the Estate. It occurs to them, for instance, that the landlord is as much dependent on them, the village, their labour, as they on him.

> "Tis true,' said Mr Forster, 'you couldn't have the land without the village.'
> 'And he can't do without the village either,' said the overseer's brother. 'He couldn't feel as happy anywhere else in this God's world than he feel on that said same hill lookin' down at us.' (p. 95.)

Because of the new mood, they haul Creighton down from God's heaven on the hill and reduce him to human proportions, on the Estate: hence they can now look at him consciously and critically, rejecting for instance his paternalism, or seeing his humanitarianism for what it really is:

> He's a nice sort of man, the landlord; he kind, he will give you if he think you really need, he's really like that, but if he got to spend any r'al sum of money, it give him heart failure. And he got more than he could ever spend in this God's world. (p. 94)

A privileged minority is the most charitable and humanitarian in any society: they possess God's own benevolence and regulate their relationship with the lower orders from Olympian heights, carrying themselves with divine aloofness. They must avoid contact, must never assume human flesh, for to be human, Lamming tells us in another beautifully realized episode involving the boys and a fisherman, is to be vulnerable. It is in this context that Creighton's anger and pain are understandable once the people not only reject his paternalism but actually show, or seem to show, disrespect to his person. Instinctively, he realizes that any personal disrespect is a challenge to the value-system that legitimizes his power over the people:

> He [the landlord] say to me sittin' in the sun beside the heap o' hay, he says we won't ever understand the kind o' responsibility he feel for you an' me an' the whole village. He say it was a real responsibility. There ain't much he can do whatever anybody may say, but he'd always feel that responsibility. We ain't his children he say, but the feelin' wus something like that. He had sort o' take care o' those who belong to the village. Things wus never as they should be, he say. He know that full well. But nothin' take away that feelin' o' responsibility he feel for you an' me an' all o' we here in this corner o' God's earth. An he say we wus lucky 'cause there be some in this islan' who never knew anybody to feel that kind of responsibility for them.

Ma, who has sympathy for the landlord and is pained by the current mood of disrespect, had gone to see him to apologize for her people's sacrilege. She is old and religious, and she is resigned to the *status quo*. She distrusts violent changes, and the future anyway is always dark and unpredictable. But her husband, Pa, infected with the new mood, rejects his wife's cautionary tale. It is Pa, gropingly, puzzled, but welcoming the new dream, who best summarizes the prevailing thoughts and attitudes:

> I ain't know exact, Ma, an' Mr Slime never so much as say except that he feel that you an' all the rest who been here donkeys years, 'tis time that we own it. If Mr Creighton an' all the Creightons from time past can own it, there ain't no reason why we mustn't. (p. 84.)

This is a revolutionary thought: what it calls for is a total overhaul of all the relations hitherto governing the island – the colonial plantocracy. Not surprisingly, some people are frightened: Ma in her religious reverence for life and continuous order, instinctively perceives the suffering attending any revolutionary changes; she fears for the children, 'the young that comin' up so fast to take the place of the old'. But most of the villagers, even when they are nervous at the daring of their own thoughts, are mesmerized by the possibilities for them and their children. Mr Slime has gained their confidence, not merely by kindling a dream where there was a vacuum, but by actually pointing at a concrete agency: a Friendly Society and a Penny Bank, which has grown in strength over a year, has shown then what their united action can achieve. The achievement of Mr Slime is this: he has given the people a measure of self-respect, a new estimation of their own worth; arising from the self-confidence regained, their imagination and thoughts rage, and like flames, reach out for other accepted notions in religion and education.

In *In the Castle of My Skin* Christianity, juxtaposed with Nature and with natural, healthy relationships between people, is seen as disrupting peoples' lives. Sometimes this brings about comic situations like that of Jan, Jen, and Susie. Jan, who has been living happily with Susie, is suddenly converted to a religious sect led by Brother Bannister, who really wants Jan for his daughter Jen. Jan makes Jen pregnant and his troubles start with Brother Bannister threatening to shoot him if he does not marry his daughter, and Susie swearing to poison herself should he desert her for another. At his wits' end, Jan promises to marry each at a different church but on the same day, at the same hour, and escapes his dilemma on the wedding day by climbing up a tree on a graveyard half-way between the two churches where he 'sit all day the day before, turn' his mind now this way, now that, like a fowl feather in the wind'. But sometimes a similar situation ends in tragedy, as in the case of Bambi, Bots and Bambina. Bambi has been living with the two women in the same house for years – there is a happy *ménage à trois*. The two women have children by him and 'everybody says they never know in all village from top to bottom a set of people who live in love an' harmony like Bots, Bambina an' Bambi, with the children'. Then a German woman comes to live in the village and persuades Bambi to 'legally' marry one of the women. They each toss a coin, he marries Bots and they all continue living as before, but the strain of a legal contract brings a psychological change in Bambi, who starts beating the women indiscriminately. This results in a complete break-up of the *ménage à trois*, and of their lives.

But apart from its destructive effects on individual lives, Lamming shows us how Christian values legitimize colonial authority, spiritually emasculating a whole community. A rejection of Creighton's domination is hence preceded by a questioning rejection of religion and Christian teachings:

They turn us dotish with all these nancy stories 'bout born again, an' we never ever give ourself a chance to get up an' get. Nothin' ain't goin' change here til we sort o' stop payin' notice to that sort o' joke 'bout a old man goin' born again. It ain't only stupid but it sound kind o' hasty,

an' that's what Mr Slime want to put an end to. He mention that said
same thing last night in the speech. An' he call it tomfoolery. 'Tis what
got us as we is, he say. (p. 136.)

Not only Christianity. The shoemaker and his friends now question the
kind of education Lamming depicts in the first section of the novel. But
they can only grope in the dark slowly. Some, like the shoemaker, who
have read bits from newspapers can just begin to glimpse at the connection
between education and power and try to pass on the knowledge to their
ignorant brethren. When Forster and Bob's father, for instance, argue that
Barbados has the best education,

> 'But if you look good,' said the shoemaker 'if you remember good, you'll
> never remember that they ever tell us 'bout Marcus Garvey. They never
> even tell us that they wus a place where we live call Africa. An' the night
> that he spoke there in the Queen's Park an' elsewhere, I see a certain
> teacher in that said high school walk from the meeting.'
> 'Why he walk out for?'
> 'Cause he didn't like Garvey tellin' him 'bout he's any brother.' The
> overseer's brother said . . .
> "Tain't no joke,' the shoemaker said, 'if you tell half of them that
> work in those places they have something to do with Africa they's piss
> straight in your face'.
> 'But why you goin' to tell men that for,' said Mr Forster, 'why tell a
> man he's somebody brother when he ain't?'
> 'That's what I mean,' the shoemaker said, 'that's just what I mean'.

That these things are being discussed at the market square where before
men met to discuss gossip from across the road is itself a sign of the change
that demands even more changes.

Two views of change run side by side in their awakened consciousness:
some, like the shoemaker, see change as an eternal theme of nature and
hence inescapable; the community should therefore ally itself with the
positive forces, for 'if times goes on changin', changin', an' we here don't
make a change one way or the next, 'tis simply a matter that times will go
along 'bout it business an' leave we all here still waitin'.' Even their knowledge of history, albeit limited, seems to prove their point: there was once
Alexander the Great; where is he now? Then there was Caesar and the
'great big' Roman Empire, the Portuguese and Spanish colonial empires;
these too had eventually crumbled. In the same way, the British Empire
would surely collapse:

God don't like ugly, an' whenever these big great empires starts to get
ugly with thing they does the Almighty puts his hand down once an'
for all. He tell them without talkin', fellows, you had your day. (p.
100.)

There are others who argue differently. To them, all the convolutions of
history are mere superficialities. When Pa becomes enthusiastic over Mr
Slime's schemes of emigration to America, Ma reminds him of his (Pa's)
emigration to Panama, and his present still poor circumstances. In the
same way, the present generation will go to America and come back 'an'
they'll sit under the lamp-post an' say night after night what an' what
they use to do'. It will be different, argues Pa, for in America money
flows faster than the flood. She counters

'Twill be the same all over again, Pa. Money come an' money go, an
'tis a thing that move through yuh fingers as the said same water you
talk about. (p. 83.)

Mr Slime's strength lies in his ability to harmonize these warring views
into a vision embodying people's deepest aspirations. To the villagers he
is a new Moses leading them to a Jerusalem where they can have better
houses and permanently own their plots of land; hence they are ready to
endure thirst and hunger across the desert. For instance they know little
about the details of the strike in town and in the village, but it is enough
that Mr Slime had spoken with the shipping authorities and had made it
clear they were not to return till he had judged the conditions satisfactory.

The strike is led by the urban workers. They have greater social and
political awareness than the villagers – a phenomenon true of most colonial
revolts. But the aggressive mood generated by the strike infects the whole
country.[4] In Creighton village, schools are closed for the day; trade and
work stops; there is expectation in the air. We view the drama in town
through the eyes of the village. Again they don't quite understand what is
happening; rumours that fighting has broken out in the town add to their
fear. The taut atmosphere, confusion and fear is caught in Lamming's
short sentences, reporting as if he was both inside and outside the people's
hearts:

There was a kind of terror in the air. The villagers were quiet and
frightened within. The sun came out and dispersed the rain clouds and
soon it was bright all over the land. All the shops were closed. The
school was closed. In the houses they tried to imagine what the fighting

was like. They had never heard of anything like it before. They had known a village fight and they were used to fights between boys and girls. Sometimes after the cricket competition one village team for various reasons might threaten to fight with the opponent. These fights made sense, but the incidents in the city were simply beyond them. There was fighting in the city. That was all they were told, and they repeated the words and tried to guess who were fighting whom. But they couldn't follow it clearly. It wasn't Mr Forster or Bots' father or the overseer's brother who were fighting. It was simply the fighting. They were fighting in the city. And the fighting would spread in the village. That was all clear. And they couldn't say they understood that. (p. 193.)

Gradually we learn what has happened in the city. A crowd of waterfront workers sent a delegation to the Governor. The sentries would not allow the delegation to pass. Hence fighting breaks out during which the police fire at the crowd and kill Po, a small boy. Rioting spreads in the town and into the surrounding villages. The peasants resent the town people, but watch with breathless expectation as the workers ambush Mr Creighton, who is saved from death by the timely arrival of Mr Slime. Disappointed, because they wanted to avenge Po's death, the men disperse. Soon the police arrive at the village with rifles and 'bayonets shining dull and deadly in the night' and things return to 'normal'.

Has anything happened? We are told, ironically, I think, that the years have changed nothing. The riots are not repeated, but things are clearly never the same again in the village. For the boy-hero, his immediate world has gradually withered away: 'where you wus sittin' wus a worl' all by itself, an' you got to get up an' go to the other world where the new something happen.' The break-up of the old is an inevitable process of growing up and what the boy uncomfortably feels – that he is seeing things for the last time – is part of the transition from adolescence to manhood. But his transition coincides with, or is a symbol of, a deeper historical experience the village community is about to undergo: the further dispossession of the peasants, thus adding them to the army of the rootless urban workers. This experience, as in many events in Lamming's novels, has a peculiar irony: the final dispossession logically follows their own agitation and their awakened consciousness. The strike and the riots make Creighton depart from the Estate; he sells the land to the Penny Bank and the Friendly Society. The people with the most shares get the first choice in the purchase of land and the house plots. These are lawyers, teachers, doctors and members of the legislative Assembly – in a word, the emergent national **bourgeoisie**.

'Tell me', the shoemaker said (when given verbal notice to quit his home by the new owner) 'what sort o' nancy story you tell me 'bout you buy this lan'; how the bloody hell you can buy this, who sell it to you, where you get money to buy it from, since when you an' a white landlord is friends for him to call you in secret an' sell you a spot o' land that I been on for only God knows how long. This ol' shop been here for more'n twenty years, an' you come on a big bright morning, like this to tell one some shitting story 'bout this spot belonging to you . . .' (p. 246.)

His incredulous outburst and protesting gestures are futile; he sobs loudly; he was one of the first and the most consistent followers of Mr Slime; he is painfully conscious of the irony that he, and the other peasants, had put 'signature' to a warrant for their exile. To emphasize that the process we are witnessing is the dispossession of the peasantry, the central importance of land is stressed over and over again.

Houses were built and houses were sold in all parts of the island. But it was different with land. This thing which stretched high and low and naked under the eye, the foot, the wind and the rain had always seemed to carry a secret buried somewhere beneath its black surface. Why did people respect land as they did? He didn't understand, but it was a kind of visitation that assisted or terrified, an infectious disease which money made imperative for the rich to inherit. The poor understood the same issue in a different way; since they couldn't own it, they rooted themselves into it. Dirt was cheap as the villagers often said, and sand was free; but land was the land, priceless, perennial and a symbol of some inexplicable power.

In this clash in which the peasants are exploited and dispossessed, turned into urban labourers even, we can hear echoes of a similar process in African and Latin America. The implacable power of money in this process and in destroying personal relationships is constantly emphasized. The feudal colonial relationship – Creighton's paternal 'responsibility' and the peasants' customary rights – is finished. Above all, cash now regulates personal relations inside the village. This is painfully brought home to us when the headmaster, a man who is respected in the village as the teacher of 'our' children and who is looked upon as a moral guide, buys the plot of land on which Pa has lived all his life. Pa is to go to an almshouse. He accepts this with stoic dignity but asks the teacher a series of puzzled questions: Why did Mr Creighton sell the land to the teacher? What was this strong relation between Mr Slime and the landlord? The headmaster

cannot answer the questions. In fact few people involved in the break-up
can explain what is happening because it can only be explained in a historical perspective and in terms of class struggle and solidarity. In the novel
it is Trumper, who has been to America, who correctly sees the break-up
in these terms. Because he has seen racial oppression and the struggle of
Negro workers, Trumper discovers his solidarity with the oppressed back
in the village; he speaks a different language, a language which not even
the graduates of the secondary schools around can comprehend. Hearing
that Pa is going to an almshouse, Trumper sums up the general pain
current in the village:

> 'The Alms House', said Trumper, ''Tis a place he would never ever go
> on his own accord in this life. He wus too decent, Pa. Slime couldn't
> look Pa in the face if it's a question o' dignity we talkin' 'bout. But that's
> life. 'Tis the way o' the world, an' in a world o' Slimes there ain't no way
> out for those who don't know how to be slimy'. (p. 294.)

He advocates the united struggle of the dispossessed.

> 'You think they dare move all the houses?' he asked. 'If every one o' you
> refuse to pay a cent on that land, and if all o' you decide to sleep in the
> street let the government find room for you in the prison house, you
> think they dare go through with this business o' selling the land?' (p. 294.)

He speaks in terms of exploitation:

> 'Way back he [Mr Slime] promise that he'd make these people here
> owners o' this land. He tell them there wasn't nothing to prevent the
> buying this lan' and he wus right, 'cause I know for a fact that the very
> money that go in the Penny Bank an' Society buy this land in his name.
> That's what I know. Nothin' he do arn't surprise me.'
>   'There are others involved,' I said. 'I know some of them.'
>   ''Course there is,' said Trumper. 'There's always more'n one in this
> kind o' deal . . .' (p. 296.)

Trumper brings a new level of thinking to bear on the situation in the
village, in this way deepening their already awakened political consciousness. 'I am going to fight for the rights of negroes, and I'll die fighting,'
he declares. Thus with the break-up of colonial feudalism we come to the
edge of a new struggle of rootless peasants (now proletarianized, because
exiled from the land) side by side with the urban workers against both the

white colonial landlord and the emergent national bourgeoisie. The novel ends with a double exile: of the villagers from their plots, their home, their 'customary' land, their old relationships, and of G. from the village, going to Trinidad. But as in the case of Trumper, we are given hints that the moment of exile in urban industry in Trinidad, America, Britain, is also a moment of discovery of one's perspective in history and of identity of interests with one's people (or class).

In light of what has happened to the peasant masses in Africa, the West Indies, and all over the former colonial world, *In the Castle of My Skin* acquires symbolic dimensions and new prophetic importance: it is one of the great political novels in modern 'colonial' literature.

REFERENCES

1 George Lamming: *In the Castle of My Skin* (McGraw-Hill, New York, 1954), p. 2.

2 George Lamming: 'The Negro Writer and His World', *Caribbean Quarterly*, Vol. No. 2.

3 Many a West Indian writer has reacted against this kind of education – a process they see as ending in mental colonialism. Sylvia Wynter in *Hills of Hebron* has denounced the West Indian élite who in exploring the symbols of power of their rulers had become enmeshed in them and 'had fallen victims to servitude more absolute than the one imposed by guns, whips, chains and hunger'.

  And James has written: 'I began to study Latin and French, then Greek and much else. But particularly we learnt, I learnt and obeyed and taught a code, the English public-school code. Britain and her colonies and the colonial peoples. What do the British people know of what they have done there? Precious little. The colonial peoples, particularly West Indians, scarcely know themselves as yet. It has taken me a long time to begin to understand.' C. L. R. James, *Beyond a Boundary* (Hutchinson, London, 1963), p. 33.

4 The strike and social upheaval which make the central crisis in the novel and which are depicted as being part of the political consciousness in Barbados must obviously have been inspired by the series of labour and political troubles which swept across the British West Indies in the thirties. In St Kitt's sugar workers went on strike for more wages; in St Vincent, the Working Men's Association pressed for land reforms and a new constitution, while in Trinidad a mass of workers in the oil-fields rioted. The riots in Trinidad, for instance, are specifically mentioned in the novel. This period also saw the emergence of early nationalist and labour leaders like Bradshaw, Grantley Adams, Bustamente and Manley.

George Lamming and the Colonial Situation[1]

▼▼▼▼▼▼▼▼▼▼▼▼▼▼▼▼▼▼▼

Exile as a universal experience pervades Lamming's novels, the dominant theme especially in *The Emigrants* and *Of Age and Innocence*. In the book of essays on politics and culture he published in 1960, he writes:

> The exile is a universal figure. The proximity of our lives to the major issues of our time has demanded of us all some kind of involvement. Some may remain neutral; but all have, at least, to pay attention to what is going on. On the political level, we are often without the right kind of information to make argument effective; on the moral level we have to feel our way through problems for which we have no adequate reference of traditional conduct as a guide. Chaos is often, therefore, the result of our thinking and our doing. We are made to feel a sense of exile by our own inadequacy and our irrelevance in a society whose past we cannot alter and whose future is always beyond us. Idleness can easily guide us into accepting this as a condition. Sooner or later, in silence or with rhetoric, we sign a contract whose epitaph reads: To be in exile is to be alive.[2]

Here the writer is seen as standing outside the stream of history and politics; his lack of a historico-moral and political frame of reference makes him feel impotent to control society. In his novels he seems to go further, to suggest that exile – a physical removal or withdrawal from one's immediate society – is an active process, and almost necessary. Often, as in *The Emigrants*, exile is conceived as a purgatorial experience which the West Indian must undergo in order to know himself. The experience involves much suffering; many of the characters in *The Emigrant* are battered and broken, and they are not even relieved by being conscious of having attained anything – not even greater wisdom. Still, the experience is necessary: 'We got to suffer first and then come together,' a character says in *The Emigrants*.

If there is one thing England going to teach all o' we is that there ain't no place like home no matter how bad home is. But you got to pay to learn, an' believe me I may not see it but those comin' after goin' make better West Indian men for comin' up here and seein' for themselves what is what.[3]

In *In the Castle of My Skin* Trumper and even the boy-hero go into voluntary exile. When Trumper comes back, he has a better grasp and appreciation of the situation in Barbados. Exile is both a spiritual and a physical state. Emigration becomes the symbol of a struggling West Indian alienated from his past and immediate world. When Lamming says that colonialism is the very base and structure of the West Indians' cultural awareness he means this form of alienation; he, the West Indian, has been severed from his roots and he is not in political control of his new society. This, at least the first aspect, is unlike the experience of the African 'who has never been wholly severed from the cradle of continuous culture and tradition'. This has given the African his strength, while 'the brevity of the West Indian's history and the fragmentary nature of the different cultures which have combined to make something new' and 'the absolute dependence on the value implicit in that language of the coloniser,'[4] have given the West Indian here a special relationship to colonialism. This relationship he calls in another place 'an example of exile'.[5]

In this essay we suggest that there are four uses to which Lamming puts the word 'exile' in his novels: exile from history and a past style of living, from race, from class, and ultimately from self. The notions are interrelated but they are not necessarily interchangeable.

In *In the Castle of My Skin*, Pa, who represents tradition and continuity, enters into a visionary dream, looking back to a time in Africa when man was in harmony with his natural environment:

Wood work in the morning and the late at night was the way we walk the world, and no one worry what wonders take place on the top of the sky. Star in the dark and stone in the shine of the sun sideways speak nothing but a world outside our world and the two was one. Fire heat in the day time and the colour that come later to take light from the eye make small difference to my people. The children were part of the pool. Hand in water and hair 'twixt the leaves where the jungle grow great was the same thing.[6]

An idyllic picture: meant to express the essence of life from which the West Indian was severed for money and profit. But from the ashes of the middle passage a new society has been born.

The families fall to pieces and many a brother never see his sister again – nor father the son. Now there's been new combinations and those that come after make quite a different collection. So if you hear some young fool fretting about back to Africa, keep away from the invalid and don't force a passage to where you won't yet belong.[7]

But the new combinations need to make 'a backward glance' to the past, to their origins, and rescue them from the disfigurement of white tutelage. This is one of the themes in *Season of Adventure*, expressed in the image of searching for a father. Fola, the step-daughter of the commissioner of police in the (imaginary) Independent Republic of San Cristobel, after listening to the remnants of African drums in the island, suddenly becomes disturbed about her origin and wants to know who her father is, a secret her mother has never disclosed to anyone. As another character comments on the case of a boy, who this time disintegrates because he can't find his mother:

'My Jesus, Jesus, spirit,' Crim cried, 'is the biggest nat'ral thing any man want to know. Who work on who give you life? Which man you can call father however it happen, which woman you call mother whatever her past position. Is the biggest nat'ral thing.'[8]

At eighteen Fola enters a season of adventure, reaching out for the truth about her roots. Because of the search, she becomes an outsider to the comfortable, secure, middle-class world of her mother and her adopted father; the two, for instance, would not have anything to do with the drums. Through her loneliness and desperate search we are made to see that it is her parents who are really lonely and hollow within, alienated from a past they would not acknowledge.

The notion of exile from race is slightly vague but is intimately connected with history. The acceptance of one's roots in Africa makes a black person, for instance, correct the racial image – again disfigured by the whites. The ceremony of the souls in *Season of Adventure*, based on a serpent cult in West Africa, is what really starts Fola on her backward glance to a past collective experience still preserved in the steel drums. Fola, who goes through the ceremony unwillingly but pulled by a power beyond her, finds herself confronted with an experience, a return to a yesterday of her race.

Fola watched her hand; yet saw that it wasn't hers; and could not recall where she had seen that hand; from what ancient or forgotten kingdom of time past had she seen that hand! But this foreign hand emerging from the body was in her memory. It was real; yet totally beyond her recollection of any recent time.[9]

It is at times suggested that the collective experience of the past is in one's blood. Charlot, a rootless Spanish Jew, with stirring feelings for the steel band, who takes Fola to the ceremony of the souls, reminds her that she is part of the dancing women. He had once seen her dance. Shocked by his statement, she retorts:

'If you could dance,' she said. 'If only you could dance! Wouldn't it be the same?'
    'Never,' said Charlot. 'I could never be held that way. However much I'd like to feel like you, I know now I can't.'[10]

Often the notion of exile from race is something the black man discovers when living away from home, an alien in a white world. Trumper in *In the Castle of My Skin* comes back from America and startles the villagers with his talk of 'my people'. 'I didn't know it till I reach the States,' he says; his in fact is a conscious identity with an oppressed race.

'My people . . . or better, my race. 'Twus in the States I find it, an' I'm gonner keep it till they kindom come.'[11]

In America black and white confront one another across the colour-line. Influenced by mass racial and political agitation, he returns and tells 'of the frenzied gospel of racial assertion – that strange soul food gospel of the rootless outsiders of the twentieth century.'[12] While his is a conscious choice, it is also forced on him by the shock of discovery.

'But you'll become a Negro like me an' all the rest in the States an' all over the world, 'cause it ain't have nothin' to do with where you born. 'Tis what you is, a different kind o' creature. An' when you see what I tellin' you an' you become a Negro, act as you should an' don't ask Hist'ry why you is what you then see yourself to be, 'cause Hist'ry got no answers. You ain't a thing till you know it, an' that's why you an' none of you on this island is a Negro yet; but if they don't know you goin' to know . . . an' that's why I bring you here for this talk, 'cause it frighten the life out o' me to know what's goin' to happen.[13]

There are some who see, but refuse to identify themselves with 'my people', the black mass in the world, or the peasants and workers – the bottom poor – in the islands. These, mainly the professionals and intellectuals, are a group whose aspirations are to acquire the trappings of the white bourgeoisie even when they most hate that world. These are seen as exiles from history, from race, in fact, ultimately, from class.

The middle class in Lamming's novels is not seen, especially before independence, as an economic class, but they have the potentiality of becoming such, once they seize the political reins. There is the headmaster who in *In the Castle of My Skin* is revoltingly described as a leech: smooth, but also coarse.

> When Mr Forster was suffering from blood poisoning, the doctor ordered that a leech be placed on the arm. The leech crouched over the arm, bright and black, and the neighbours watched it grow fat with the intake of blood. Walking beside the Inspector towards the school the head teacher had that black slouching carriage of the leech, and when he smiled back at the Inspector the flash of his face rose as though the new intake of feeling was fattening.[14]

Even Mr Slime, who has done so much to awaken the village's consciousness, is finally depicted as being slimy, making a deal with the departing Creighton; he has betrayed the trust of the masses, and sold the people to the rising class of lawyers, doctors and teachers so that even Pa has to go to an almshouse. To this class belong people like Dickson, who in *The Emigrants* sets himself apart from the workers and their searching discussions, yet takes enormous pleasure in talking, with 'a fastidious precision', to a senile English doctor.

> He had an obsession with the principles of the language and wouldn't at the point of a gun end a sentence with a preposition . . . Later the doctor stroked him on the shoulder and made an appropriate little prophecy about his future.[15]

This class, in *Season of Adventure*, inherits political power and privileges. In fact, in the Independent Republic of San Cristobel racial origins have become hazy, and the various groupings have been polarized into two opposing camps. There is the ruling élite, corrupt, imprisoned in their social committees for everything under the sun: 'cat shows, beauty contests, volume competitions between radiograms, artist's endeavours, and any activity which attracted public notice in the capital.' There are the workers, beasts of burden, seething bitterly under a régime whose members deduct three-quarters of a worker's wages because he has spilt champagne on the master's jacket. The masses' spiritual centre is the Forest Reserve where the drum-boys play, echoing something of the people's past and voicing their present aspirations. It is to the Forest Reserve Boys that Fola runs when escaping the 'dead' middle-class background of her upbringing. In seeking her roots, she finds her class. She is an exile returning home. Her relation to the 'drum-boys' and the masses is intellectually stated by the omnipresent author. The author, relating the story of Powell who assassinates the president, suddenly breaks the narrative and inserts a note to explain his own relationship to Powell. Powell is his brother by a different mother. They lived together dreaming the same dreams:

> Identical in years, and stage by stage, Powell and I were taught in the same primary school. And then the division came, I got a public scholarship which started my migration into another world, a world whose roots were the same, but whose style of living was entirely different from that my childhood knew. It had earned me a privilege which now shut Powell and the whole *tonelle* right out of my future. And yet! Yet I forgot the *tonelle* as men forget a war. And I attached myself to this new world which was so recent and so slight beside the weight of what had gone before. Instinctively I attached myself to that new privilege; and in spite of all my effort, I am not free of its embrace, even to this day.[16]

The author's exile is not only from a class (he originally belonged to the masses), but also from tradition and race as embodied in the *tonelle*. Lamming's middle class approximates that of Frantz Fanon: Frantz Fanon says of the bourgeoisie of the developing countries:

> The national middle class which takes over power at the end of the colonial regime is an underdeveloped middle class. It has practically no economic power, and in any case it is in no way commensurate with the bourgeoisie of the mother country which it hopes to replace. In its wilful narcissism, the national middle class is easily convinced that it can advantageously replace the middle class of the mother country . . . The university and merchant classes which make up the most enlightened section of the new state are in fact characterized by the smallness of their number and their being concentrated in the capital and the type of activities in which they are engaged: business, agriculture and the liberal professions.[17]

Yet the ambivalence in the attitude of the fictional author, who feels responsible for Powell's criminal defeat and still clings to his privileges,

pervades the novels discussed; it is not quite clear what Lamming's uprooted middle class is to do beyond achieving a common broad political
front with the masses. How in any case do you return to the roots, to your
race, to your class? In a sense, Lamming gives an answer in *Season for
Adventure*, where the people revolt and a new government is installed.
The new president, Dr Beako, who as a lecturer in the University had
often insisted that 'a new Republic like San Cristobel, made backward
by a large illiterate peasantry, and weaned into complacency by a commercial middle-class that had no power in the world that organized its
money' was in a state of Emergency, would now presumably bring about
basic changes. Lamming's attempt to bring about a resolution between his
opposing classes – to show the exiled middle class the way to go home –
does not come off in *Season of Adventure* mainly because of his treatment
(we do not really enter into the lives of any of the groups) and also
because it is not in the province of a novel to give answers. Lamming
has in fact made a better exploration of exile and identity in a previous
novel, *Of Age and Innocence*, where the problems and dilemmas of the
alienated individuals (middle class mostly) are woven into the larger dilemmas and tension in the state; where San Cristobel, to a degree more
successful than in *Season of Adventure*, corresponds to an actual Caribbean
island.

Of Age and Innocence[18] like Lamming's other novels, defies neat intellectual compartments; a complex private act is intimately bound up with
an equally complex public stage; the two, while inseparable, exist in an
uneasy juxtaposition, often at war, pulling in different directions; the
moment of harmony between the private and the public is fleeting. Individuals and society, past and present, are wrought into a moving whole
which brings people into a new historical chapter: but underlying the
possibility of better prospects for the children are the unsettling memories
of yesterday.

In this novel, as in *Season of Adventure* which comes later, he has
chosen an imaginary Caribbean island, San Cristobel, as the setting. Like
John Hearne, who has invented Cayuna island for his novels, Lamming
wants to overcome the necessary limitations, political ones especially, of
using an actual territory. The practice has drawbacks, which John Hearne
and Lamming do not entirely overcome: in an actual territory a novelist
can assume a common body of historical and social beliefs and add subtle
tensions to his work by mere allusions; in an invented territory the novelist
has to explain the allusions, or early on in the story provide a body of facts,
beliefs and practices unique to it. Lamming has done the latter; he has
invented an area with a history and social make-up representative of the

Caribbean area, with its racial mixtures, as a whole. San Cristobel, we are told, is:

> No new country, but an old old island inhabiting new forms of men who can never resurrect their roots and do not know their nature. Colour is their old and only alphabet. The white are turning whites and the black are like an instinct which some voice, my voice, shall exercise.[19]

People meet to celebrate the island's past disasters, for instance they bring propitiating gifts to the sea to prevent a second occurrence of the flood that once drowned the island. The history of the island is celebrated in song and legend: the story of the Tribe Boys and how they proudly fought off a superior force of Bandit Kings. A number of things emerge from this legend.

The Island is depicted as having roots in a past harmony when:

> . . . plain animal talk, an' the fish dancing, wild an' makin' faces at the bottom o' the ocean, an' only the sun get permission to say the time, an' the moon only makin' plans to decide the size o' the sea, as makin' fun at some mountains which couldn't climb no more, an' sometimes collapse if a new tide turn upside down, and shake up the sand. Like such a time it was for San Cristobel, long, long before human interference.[20]

When the Tribe Boys arrive in the island, they fit into this harmony of nature. Under their possession, the land takes up a 'human shape', it fruitfully responds to the touch of their fingers.

> 'An' it work like a miracle in the sleep, the way thin's seem to respect them. An' it seem that what we refer to as family was not a mere man an' woman with the result thereof, but animals too. The land play human too, learn to obey, an' they had some peace.'[21]

This is essentially the way Pa in *In the Castle of My Skin* sees Africa. Only now the idyllic scene goes deep into San Cristobel's past: here is an attempt to show that the West Indies had history long before Africa, Asia and Europe came on the scene. It is this idyllic existence that the marauding bandits break.

Another thing to be noted in the legend is the exemplary course of the Tribe Boys and their desire for freedom. When finally defeated through the Bandits' cunning use of ants, the Tribe Boys, rather than surrender, all jump into the sea. Freedom is here seen as the object, and what justifies human existence.

There are obvious similarities between the legend and the modern generation who are engaged in similar struggles for freedom. The era of the Tribe Boys ended with the island sinking under the sea and then being born again. This 'historic deliverance' from water is paralleled with a second possible deliverance from colonial era. A new epoch is to be born out of the present turmoil. Resurrection, new life, innocence born of the accumulated mistakes and wisdom of ages, are recurring themes and images reinforcing Lamming's vision of a new Caribbean.

Here Africa and India shake hands with China, and Europe wrinkles like a brow begging every face to promise love. The past is all suspicion, now is an argument that will not end, and tomorrow for San Cristobel, tomorrow is like the air in your hands . . . San Cristobel so old and yet so new, no place, but a promise.[22]

The mood generated by the three leaders, Shephard, Singh and Lee, infects most people, down to an ordinary street thief who can see himself 'ridin' high', "cause time call a new tune, an' we both goin' rule San Cristobel, you an' me . . . an' every boy an' daughter born out o' the mixture we make.' The thief calls on all to forget the past racial antagonism in the struggle for freedom.

'Look me straight Baboo, an' see how skin curse the light like judgement evenin' for a soul in sin. But tomorrow comin', tomorrow near . . . an' we goin' all sing with the same no-colour smile.'[23]

The resurrection envisaged here is, in part, society's attempt to recapture the harmony of the past, the essence of life as lived by the Tribe Boys.

As in *In the Castle of My Skin*, the men who initiate the rebirth are themselves exiles: they have lived in Europe, and they are separated from their roots, traditions and class. Often they themselves are torn apart, and in attempting to resolve their personal dilemmas find themselves involved in the contradictions of their own society; their fulfilment as individuals cannot be separated from the destiny of their people.

For instance, Mark Kennedy, a writer, has lived in Europe since he was ten. After twenty years in exile he is now returning home, nervous, and isolated even amongst his friends in the plane. He shudders when the plane rocks in the air, his nerves tight.

'Remember the faces of those who died.' The words worked on his nerves with a smooth and gradual destructiveness like flakes of glass losing their way through flesh.[24]

Death haunts him; in the plane he feels how powerless an individual is, when so trapped. Lamming carefully points Mark's physical sensations to indicate the man's inner state: Mark is scared of any involvement that would place upon him, the individual, any demands. His English girl-friend, Marcia, accuses him of not wanting to 'feel any responsibility, not even to me'. In London, for instance, he would not make arrangements with her about their living together; he even chose unpredictable hours to visit her, because this gave him 'the feeling that he was still on his own'. Even a gesture of sympathy from Marcia in the plane appears 'like an act of intrusion'. His lack of involvement springs from a spiritual inertia, what he calls a disinclination to act, even to communicate. He writes in his diaries:

Is this failure to communicate a kind of illness which puts me out of touch with the others? I have looked for it in them, and I am suddenly made feeble by their fluency. I try to find a way which would enable others to enter my secret so that they might, through a common ex-perience, lead me to its source. But my effort moves off the mark. I begin as it were, from the circumference of my meaning, moving cautiously and with loyal feeling, towards a centre which very soon I discover I cannot reach. Then speech deserts me. I abandon what I had felt to be an obligation, and the result is silence.[25]

What overpowers him is the dislocation he finds between objects, even people; dislocation between the inward and the outward, between desire and action. In another entry in his diary, he records his experience on a beach with a pebble, a piece of iron, and a dead crab. It is the very absence of a discernible relationship between the objects that restores individuality to each.

A certain lack of connection had endowed the pebble with a formidable and determined power of its presence. It was there, independent, obsti-nate, decisive.[26]

He is fascinated by the unique splendour of the pebble, just as Sartre's Antoine in *Nausea* is disgusted by a single pebble on the beach and attracted by a piece of paper. He wants to touch it but is further attracted by a piece of rusty iron which appears 'dejected, and wore its rust like a mark of humiliation, which it had completely overcome, a ruined memory of the black earth from which it had come.' Again he fails to touch it, his attention having been caught by 'a questioning dead eye of the crab' which he desires to crush. He lifts his hand, but like Antoine,[27] he cannot: 'I felt my fingers fall in a willed reluctance to the sand,' he writes:

> This feeling of disinclination surrounds me like space, it enters me like air. It is like my hand which reminds me of the distance between me and the object it brings me in contact with. I can feel it like a clutch around my throat, an annihilation of things about me, a sudden and natural dislocation of meaning. And it is no force other than me which moves me. It is me.[28]

Mark is an existential hero, aware of his individual existence, and like Camus' hero in *L'Etranger*, will not be involved in a willed action or in 'normal' emotions of pity, love, regret or hatred. People, objects exist, yes, but life has no meaning other than the individual's continual freedom to choose.

> Freedom and Death, like opposites and contradictions working in harmony, are the two facts which we cannot bargain, the two great facts, Freedom and Death, twin gods or forces or whatever you like which haunt every human existence. Beyond these is nothing but the infinite and indefinable background against which we ramble in the service of Freedom and the expectation of Death. But here we can choose. And our choice is not complete until it becomes an act, for it is only action which can help us out of error . . . and only through the discovery of error that we may be able to define some truth . . .[29]

But although Mark has his counterparts in the alienated hero of French literature (note for instance the overpowering consciousness of death in Simone de Beauvoir's book *Force of Circumstance*), his alienation is connected with his colonial status. He is separated from the continuing life in the island, uprooted from its age-old customs and from those of his other ancestors from Africa, and is not politically involved. The only time he speaks to a crowd, he feels, for the first time, very close to a communal spirit with roots in the soil. He evokes this spirit of belonging to the land with a great nostalgic power of exile.

> Nationalism is not only frenzy and struggle with all its necessary demand for the destruction of those forces which condemn you to the status we call colonial. The national spirit is deeper and more enduring than that. It is original and necessary as the root to the body of the tree. It is the private feeling you experience of possessing and being possessed by the

whole landscape of the place where you were born, the freedom which helps you to recognize the rhythm of the winds, the silence and aroma of the night, rocks, water, pebble and branch, animal and bird noise, the temper of the sea and the mornings arousing nature everywhere to the silent and sacred communion between you and the roots you have made in this island. It is in the bond between each man and that corner of the earth which his birth and his work have baptised with the name, home.[30]

In his speech Mark is inspired by the earliest memories of the island, particularly the legend of the Tribe Boys and the Bandit Kings; their choice of death is the supreme affirmation of freedom. But although Mark articulates his dilemma and argues that choice is not complete until it becomes an act, he still remains the uninvolved individual; this vivid experience of the crowd, his one moment of real contact, only affirms his existential self: I exist.

The crowd was a frozen presence which hardened his identity. He existed. Mark Kennedy existed. No force could ever alter that private experience which the crowd had now made sacred. His existence, like death, was a fact. This was a knowledge beyond argument, independent of reason, absolute, irreversible. He had chosen the legend of the Tribe Boys by chance, but his speech was a certainty which he could not really share. He had been talking to himself. His speech was a fragment of dialogue between Mark Kennedy and himself, and the theme was identity.[31]

Can an individual in society choose not to act? Is the refusal to act not itself a form of action which can unleash a chain of reactions? In this novel, Mark's verbal assurance of love, a belated attempt to heal the wound, reverberates with fatigue and failure.

The destructive individuality of Mark is sharply contrasted with the creative energy of Shephard, who transcends his divided self in an unswerving pursuit of his, and the island's identity. He is a man of passion whose words, we are told, 'were spoken from a depth of torture and delight, and his face, like a lost piece of night carving its image upon the afternoon, was the face of a fugitive who had meandered through all weathers to a season of insanity.' Through this passion he awakens San Cristobel to a new conception of itself, so that everybody speaks as if 'they had discovered a new dimension in time'. People understand him because his words closely describe their social situation and experiences; in his passionate commitment to a vision, he recreates the people's dreams:

'He move my heart that morning,' the woman said, 'an' if I could have lay my han' on them who say he was mad, only if I could have lay my han' on the lyn' tongue that try to slander his brain.'

'They didn't want him to do the work he start' the man said, 'but he choose the right day to make that speech, the mornin' we celebrate San Cristobel. 'Tis a next day o' deliverance he goin' bring.'

'And he ain't talk no lies' the woman said, 'he ain't let his tongue slip a single lie when he say that San Cristobel is his an' mine, an' how he goin' make it belong to everybody who born here.'[32]

Like Mark, Shephard has been away in Europe. As children the two grew up together, steeped in the island's legends. Playing with Mark, Shephard, even as a child, is shown as having powerful imagination. Shephard, like Mark, is an exile, an alienated individual, who returns home in search of his roots, his identity.

He is, at first, ashamed of himself, of his colour. In his diary Mark writes about Shephard:

Can it be that Shephard has always been in part afraid or ashamed to see himself? I ask this question of Shephard and at the same time I feel it is a question I have also put in silence to myself.[33]

In the same entry Mark records their conversation in which Shephard tries to explain this general sense of shame. Shephard says of England:

I felt surrounded by a perpetual act of persecution. I was judged finally by the evidence which my body, a kind of professional spy, always offered. And there were times when I have felt my presence utterly built up by the glance which another had given me. I wanted to disappear or die. I don't think I have always had this feeling but I was aware of it for the first time in England.[34]

In being ashamed of another man's glance, Shephard is rejecting himself. This feeling, of course, stems from the fact that colour, in a white-dominated society, has moral attributes and is used as a criterion of man's worth. Nevertheless this feeling is shown to be general and can arise when society, for instance, rejects any group of people on basis of certain natural attributes it does not approve of. Penelope, a white girl, is driven to isolation, even from her friends, the moment she discovers her lesbian desire for Marcia. Penelope is engaged to Bill and together with Mark and Marcia have lived more or less closely in England, and even in San Cristobel.

Mark's brutal treatment of Marcia kindles Penelope's protective instincts, which turn into a lesbian lust. If she confesses, she argues with herself, will her friends not start to reconsider her, to accept her with reservations? Her status would be altered, she would carry the mark of the beast – 'the measure of her fall from the general order'.

It would be better to lose one's status completely and be seen wholly as a new thing; much better than to have one's status granted with a new reservation. It is the reservation which occupies the mind of the other, until one feels it like a scar, or a defamation. I believe this is what those people who are called inferior experience and find resentful and intolerable. . . . The Negro, the homosexual, the Jew, the worker . . . he is a man, that is never denied, but he is not quite ready for definition until these reservations are stated, and it is the reservation which separates him from himself.[35]

The reservation can separate 'him from himself' and also from society. So can a secret. Bob, Lee, Singh and Rowley, four children who represent the four communities – African, Chinese, Indian, English – have forged a non-racial society which keeps the children apart from their warring fathers. They share the island's legends, the harmony between them is almost complete. But each one suddenly discovers a secret in himself which he cannot possibly share with the others, and this feeling of shame slightly alienates each from the group. Towards the end of the novel we are shown how the various characters, even those linked by ties of race, traditions, respect or friendship, are possessed, in varying degrees, by this feeling of alienation, because they cannot possibly share their secret guilts and knowledge.

'Secrets,' writes Penelope, 'are difficult to conceal because a secret is by nature contagious. It confronts you with such dubious isolation; it makes a special exception of you; it modifies your relation with everybody else.'[36]

Alienation seems to be a human condition, though for the West Indian it stems from his specific position as a colonial. But when a man discovers this condition in himself and the specific factors that give rise to it he can have a deeper human contact with other people. Penelope for instance is able to understand Shephard.

'To be Shephard in spite of . . .' (the broken images go through her in a flash of human identity) 'To be Penelope in spite of . . . To be a man in spite of . . .' The phrases stood out like the origin and end of all her understanding. In spite of . . . in spite of . . . she raised her body from the blanket and held her hand out. She wanted to go, but she wanted him to know that she understood this feeling which had disfigured his innocence and separated him from himself.[37]

Previously she and the others had thought him mad because he had held their plane and threatened people with a pistol, pouring a torrent of abuse and hate on Penelope. Now he explains, and she understands, that in her he had seen another woman who, in England, had rejected him and consequently made him aware of his alienation. Mark too can understand Shephard because in him Mark can see himself. Retrospectively, he explains the act in the plane in terms of alienation – exile from self.

No one could escape. There was nearness of disaster so that the eyes which saw him could not afford to be casual. They had to look. And that was what he wanted. He wanted to be looked at as he occupied the centre of that world's attention. He wanted to rob his mind of its concern for the others' regard, and he tried to do this by making his body serve as a real traitor.[38]

Shephard's response to his 'divided self' indicates the real difference between him and Mark. For a time in England he hides away in guilt and secrecy, afraid to accept himself and his racial origins. Now he accepts his negritude and finds his solidarity with the masses.

My rebellion [he tells Penelope] begins with an acceptance of the very thing I reject, because my conduct cannot have the meaning I want to give it, if it does not accept and live through that conception by which the others now regard it. What I may succeed in doing is changing that conception. But I cannot ignore it.[39]

Mark is an intellectual whose ability to see so well paralyses him; Shephard sees through his passion, acts when he sees, and sees because he acts. He goes into politics, he says so himself, in order to redefine himself through action. Political involvement in the fight for freedom is seen as the only way a community and individuals in it can find their roots. But discovery of one's exile, even a society's, is a necessary step. Crabbe, the head of the police, can see clearly what Shephard is doing even though he does not understand Shephard's motivation.

He wanted each group to get an idea of who they were and that must include where they originally came from. When he had planted that in their heads once and for all, what did he do next? He showed them that there was no difference between them, Indian, Negro, Chinese, or what you like, in their relation to people like me and the Governor and what he calls the fellows at White Hall. That's what he made clear and isn't a soul in San Cristobel, literate or illiterate, young or old, who didn't understand what he was saying. Whatever difference there was between them, they had one thing in common: a colonial past with all that it implies.[40]

Thus awareness of the loneliness of the individual, self-awareness of one's exile, are not enough. For Lamming a sense of exile must lead to action, and through action to identity. The West Indian's alienation springs not from his immediate confrontation with machines, not even from being in an industrial mass society, but from his colonial relationship to England. Political freedom as a necessary condition before the West Indian can find himself is one controlling spirit in Lamming's novel. The relationship between the national bourgeoisie and the mass of peasants and workers is the other. As independence approaches in the West Indies, the latter relationship becomes even more important and dominates the last novel: *Season of Adventure*. But in all the novels, any movement in search of identity must be based on the masses: the élite must accept responsibility for the community as a whole; all must help in building a new society. What Lamming's society is to be like is not clear. But in *Of Age and Innocence* the symbol of his new society is that of the three boys who find their solidarity with Rowley. The novel ends with them going to mourn Rowley's death, oblivious of the rivalries and hatred of their elders. The children are Innocence where Ma Shephard is Age – continuity and tradition. They are the spirit of resurrection, a new West Indian awareness born out of the necessary political turmoil of the past.

Lamming, however, does not simplify: he knows the vicissitudes of human behaviour, the criss-crossing of human motives and action. Crabbe and Paravenco, vying with one another, playing a cat and mouse game for the Governor's favours, are a well delineated pair of bankrupt and hungry politicians in relentless pursuit of personal power and gain. Even Shephard is shown as being perilously close to a lust for power and in danger of using people as pawns. Daboo, who murders Shephard so that Singh, 'an Indian like myself', can inherit power, finds his leader immobile with anger: he has done the very thing Singh would have died to stop. Daboo's cry at the feet of the deeply shocked Singh is a despairing one of loneliness and mistaken motives:

> Was only for you, Singh, was only for you. I do it, from infancy I dream to see someone like myself, some Indian with your achievement rule San Cristobel. My only mistake was to wish it for you, Singh, was only for you I do what I do.[41]

There is cruel irony in the words.

REFERENCES

1 Presented at the Thirteenth Annual Meeting of the African Studies Association, Boston, October 21–24, 1970.
2 George Lamming: *The Pleasures of Exile* (Joseph, London, 1960), p. 24.
3 George Lamming: *The Emigrants* (Joseph, London, 1954), p. 77.
4 *The Pleasures of Exile*, p. 34.
5 *The Pleasures of Exile*, p. 156.
6 George Lamming: *In the Castle of My Skin* (McGraw-Hill, New York, 1954), p. 215.
7 *In the Castle of My Skin*, p. 215.
8 George Lamming: *Season of Adventure* (Joseph, London, 1960), p. 92.
9 *Season of Adventure*, p. 44.
10 *Season of Adventure*, p. 28.
11 *In the Castle of My Skin*, p. 304.
12 Richard Wright: Introduction to the American Edition of *In the Castle of My Skin* (McGraw-Hill, New York, 1954)
13 *In the Castle of My Skin*, p. 306.
14 *In the Castle of My Skin*, p. 33.
15 George Lamming: *The Emigrants*, p. 59.
16 *Season of Adventure*, p. 102.
17 Franz Fanon: *The Wretched of the Earth*, (Penguin, London, 1967), pp. 119–120. Word for word, what he says of the class would apply to the world of Lamming's novels.
18 George Lamming: *Of Age and Innocence* (Joseph, London, 1958).
19 *Of Age and Innocence*, p. 58.
20 *Of Age and Innocence*, p. 95.
21 *Of Age and Innocence*, p. 96.
22 *Of Age and Innocence*, p. 58.
23 *Of Age and Innocence*, p. 80.
24 *Of Age and Innocence*, p. 27.
25 *Of Age and Innocence*, p. 110.
26 *Of Age and Innocence*, p. 72.
27 Jean-Paul Sartre: *Nausea* (Penguin edition). Antoine Roquentin also writes and is interested in the individuality of objects. A pebble disgusts him (p. 10 and p. 22) and he starts to pick up a piece of paper: 'I bent

down, already looking forward to touching this fresh and tender pulp which would roll into grey balls in my fingers. . . . I couldn't do it.' (p. 22). Of objects he writes: 'I am afraid of entering in contact with them, just as if they were living animals.' (p. 22).

28 *Of Age and Innocence*, p. 73.
29 *Of Age and Innocence*, p. 174.
30 *Of Age and Innocence*, p. 175.
31 *Of Age and Innocence*, p. 179.
32 *Of Age and Innocence*, p. 77.
33 *Of Age and Innocence*, p. 111.
34 *Of Age and Innocence*, p. 112.
35 *Of Age and Innocence*, p. 151.
36 *Of Age and Innocence*, p. 149.
37 *Of Age and Innocence*, p. 206.
38 *Of Age and Innocence*, p. 113.
39 *Of Age and Innocence*, p. 204.
40 *Of Age and Innocence*, p. 167.
41 *Of Age and Innocence*, p. 384.

APPENDIX

On the Abolition of the English Department[1]

▼▼▼▼▼▼▼▼▼▼▼▼▼▼▼▼▼▼▼▼▼▼▼▼▼▼▼▼▼▼▼▼▼

1. This is a comment on the paper presented by the Acting Head of the English Department at the University of Nairobi to the 42nd meeting of the Arts Faculty Board on the 20th September, 1968.

2 (a) That paper was mainly concerned with possible developments within the Arts Faculty and their relationship with the English Department, particularly:

   (i) The place of modern languages, especially French;

  (ii) The place and role of the Department of English;

 (iii) The emergence of a Department of Linguistics and Languages;

 (iv) The place of African languages, especially Swahili.

(b) In connection with the above, the paper specifically suggested that a department of Linguistics and Languages, to be closely related to English, be established.

(c) A remote possibility of a Department of African literature, or alternatively, that of African literature and culture, was envisaged.

3. The paper raised important problems. It should have been the subject of a more involved debate and discussion, preceding the appointment of a committee with specific tasks, because it raises questions of value, direction and orientation.

4. For instance, the suggestions, as the paper itself admits, question the role and status of an English Department in an African situation and environment. To quote from his paper:

The English Department has had a long history at this College and has built up a strong syllabus which by its study of the *historic continuity of a single culture throughout the period of emergence of the modern west*, makes it an important companion to History and to Philosophy and

Religious Studies. However, *it is bound to become less 'British', more open to other writing in English (American, Caribbean, African, Commonwealth) and also to continental writing, for comparative purposes.*

5. Underlying the suggestions is a basic assumption that the English tradition and the emergence of the modern west is the central root of our consciousness and cultural heritage. Africa becomes an extension of the west, an attitude which, until a radical reassessment, used to dictate the teaching and organization of History in our University.[2] Hence, in fact, the assumed centrality of English Department, into which other cultures can be admitted from time to time, as fit subjects for study, or from which other satellite departments can spring as time and money allow. A small example is the current, rather apologetic attempt to smuggle African writing into an English syllabus in our three colleges.

6. Here then, is our main question: If there is need for a 'study of the historic continuity of a single culture', why can't this be African? Why can't African literature be at the centre so that we can view other cultures in relationship to it?

This is not mere rhetoric: already African writing, with the sister connections in the Caribbean and the Afro-American literatures, has played an important role in the African renaissance, and will become even more and more important with time and pressure of events. Just because for reasons of political expediency we have kept English as our official language, there is no need to substitute a study of English culture for our own. We reject the primacy of English literature and culture.

7. The aim, in short, should be to orientate ourselves towards placing Kenya, East Africa, and then Africa in the centre. All other things are to be considered in their relevance to our situation, and their contribution towards understanding ourselves.

8. We therefore suggest:

   A. That the English Department be abolished;
   B. That a Department of African Literature and Languages be set up in its place.

The primary duty of any literature department is to illuminate the spirit animating a people, to show how it meets new challenges, and to investigate possible areas of development and involvement.

In suggesting this name, we are not rejecting other cultural streams, especially the western stream. We are only clearly mapping out the directions and perspectives the study of culture and literature will inevitably take in an African university.

9. We know that European literatures constitute one source of influence

on modern African literatures in English, French, and Portuguese; Swahili, Arabic, and Asian literatures constitute another, an important source, especially here in East Africa; and the African tradition, a tradition as active and alive as ever, constitutes the third and the most significant. This is the stuff on which we grew up, and it is the base from which we make our cultural take-off into the world.

10. Languages and linguistics should be studied in the department because in literature we see the principles of languages and linguistics in action. Conversely, through knowledge of languages and linguistics we can get more from literature. For linguistics not to become eccentric, it should be studied in the Department of African Literature and Languages.

In addition to Swahili, French, and English, whenever feasible other languages such as Arabic, Hindustani, Kikuyu, Luo, Akamba, etc., should be introduced into the syllabus as optional subjects.

11. On the literature side, the Department ought to offer roughly:
   (a) The oral tradition, which is our primary root;
   (b) Swahili literature (with Arabic and Asian literatures): this is another root, especially in East Africa;
   (c) A selected course in European literature: yet another root;
   (d) Modern African literature.

For the purposes of the Department, a knowledge of Swahili, English, and French should be compulsory. The largest body of writing by Africans is now written in the French language. Africans writing in the French language have also produced most of the best poems and novels. In fact it makes nonense to talk of modern African literature without French.

12. *The Oral Tradition*

The Oral tradition is rich and many-sided. In fact 'Africa is littered with Oral Literature'. But the art did not end yesterday; it is a living tradition. Even now there are songs being sung in political rallies, in churches, in night clubs by guitarists, by accordion players, by dancers, etc. Another point to be observed is the interlinked nature of art forms in traditional practice. Verbal forms are not always distinct from dance, music, etc. For example, in music there is close correspondence between verbal and melodic tones; in 'metrical lyrics' it has been observed that poetic text is inseparable from tune; and the 'folk tale' often bears an 'operatic' form, with sung refrain as an integral part. The distinction between prose and poetry is absent or very fluid.

Though tale, dance, song, myth, etc. can be performed for individual aesthetic enjoyment, they have other social purposes as well. Dance, for example, has been studied 'as symbolic expression of social reality reflecting and influencing the social, cultural and personality systems of which it is a part'. The oral tradition also comments on society because of its intimate relationship and involvement.

The study of the oral tradition at the University should therefore lead to a multi-disciplinary outlook: literature, music, linguistics, Sociology, Anthropology, History, Psychology, Religion, Philosophy. Secondly, its study can lead to fresh approaches by making it possible for the student to be familiar with art forms different in kind and historical development from Western literary forms. Spontaneity and liberty of communication inherent in oral transmission – openness to sounds, sights, rhythms, tones, in life and in the environment – are examples of traditional elements from which the student can draw. More specifically, his familiarity with oral literature could suggest new structures and techniques; and could foster attitudes of mind characterized by the willingness to experiment with new forms, so transcending 'fixed literary patterns' and what that implies – the preconceived ranking of art forms.

The study of the Oral Tradition would therefore supplement (not replace) courses in Modern African Literature. By discovering and proclaiming loyalty to indigenous values, the new literature would on the one hand be set in the stream of history to which it belongs and so be better appreciated; and on the other be better able to embrace and assimilate other thoughts without losing its roots.

13. *Swahili Literature*

There is a large amount of oral and written classical Swahili Literature of high calibre. There is also a growing body of modern Swahili literature: both written and oral.

14. *European Literature*

Europe has influenced Africa, especially through English and French cultures. In our part of Africa there has been an over-concentration on the English side of European life. Even the French side, which is dominant in other countries of Africa, has not received the importance it deserves. We therefore urge for freedom of choice so that a more representative course can be drawn up. We see no reason why English literature should have priority over and above other European literatures where we are concerned. The Russian novel of the nineteenth century should and must be taught. Selections from American, German, and other European literatures should also be introduced. In other words English writings will be taught in their European context and only for their relevance to the East African perspective.

15. *Modern African Literature*

The case for the study of Modern African Literature is self-evident. Its possible scope would embrace:

(a) The African novel written in French and English;

(b) African poetry written in French and English, with relevant translations of works written by Africans in Portuguese and Spanish;

(c) The Caribbean novel and poetry: the Caribbean involvement with Africa can never be over-emphasized. A lot of writers from the West Indies have often had Africa in mind. Their works have had a big impact on the African renaissance – in politics and literature. The poetry of Negritude indeed cannot be understood without studying its Caribbean roots. We must also study Afro-American literuture.

16. *Drama*

Since drama is an integral part of literature, as well as being its extension, various dramatic works should be studied as parts of the literature of the people under study. Course in play-writing, play-acting, directing, lighting, costuming, etc. should be instituted.

17. *Relationship with other Departments*

From things already said in this paper, it is obvious that African Oral and Modern literatures cannot be fully understood without some understanding of social and political ideas in African history. For this, we propose that either with the help of other departments, or within the department, or both, courses on mutually relevant aspects of African thought be offered. For instance, an introductory course on African art – sculpture, painting – could be offered in co-operation with the Department of Design and Architecture.

18. The 3.1.1[3] should be abolished. We think an undergraduate should be exposed to as many general ideas as possible. Any specialization should come in a graduate school where more specialized courses can be offered.

19. In other words we envisage an active Graduate School will develop, which should be organized with such departments as the Institute for Development studies.

20. *Conclusion*

One of the things which has been hindering a radical outlook in our study of literature in Africa is the question of literary excellence; that only works of undisputed literary excellence should be offered. (In this case it meant virtually the study of disputable 'peaks' of English literature.) The question of literary excellence implies a value judgement as to what is literary and what is excellence, and from whose point of view. For any group it is better to study representative works which mirror their society rather than to study a few isolated 'classics', either of their own or of a foreign culture.

To sum up, we have been trying all along to place values where they belong. We have argued the case for the abolition of the present Department of English in the College, and the establishment of a Department of

African Literature and Languages. This is not a change of names only. We want to establish the centrality of Africa in the department. This, we have argued, is justifiable on various grounds, the most important one being that education is a means of knowledge about ourselves. Therefore, after we have examined ourselves, we radiate outwards and discover peoples and worlds around us. With Africa at the centre of things, not existing as an appendix or a satellite of other countries and literatures, things must be seen from the African perspective. The dominant object in that perspective is African literature, the major branch of African culture. Its roots go back to past African literatures, European literatures, and Asian literatures. These can only be studied meaningfully in a Department of African Literature and Languages in an African University.

We ask that this paper be accepted in principle; we suggest that a representative committee be appointed to work out the details and harmonize the various suggestions into an administratively workable whole.

James Ngugi
Henry Owuor-Anyumba
Taban Lo Liyong
24th October 1968

REFERENCES

1 This debate resulted in the establishment of two departments: Languages and Literature. In both, African languages and literature were to form the core. In the case of the Literature Department, Caribbean and black American literature were to be emphasized. It thus represents a radical departure in the teaching of literature in Africa.

2 Then University of East Africa with three constituent colleges at Makerere, Dar es Salaam, and Nairobi. Since then the three have become autonomous universities.

3 This is a course for those who want to specialize in literature: 1st year – three subjects; 2nd and 3rd years – literature only.

Index